EAST ANGLIAN
DAILY TIMES

IPSWICH TOWN FC
The 1970s – The Glory Years Begin

WOULD YOU LIKE ONE OF THE IMAGES IN THIS BOOK?

To order a copy of any of the classic photographs within this book, and to view many others, go to www.eadt.co.uk/myphotos24 or telephone Sharon Clark on 01473 324813

EAST ANGLIAN DAILY TIMES

EveningStar

IPSWICH TOWN FC

The 1970s – The Glory Years Begin

FOREWORD BY MICK MILLS   TERRY HUNT

DB PUBLISHING

First published in Great Britain in 2010 by
The Derby Books Publishing Company Limited,
3 The Parker Centre, Derby, DE21 4SZ.

This paperback edition published in Great Britain in 2014 by DB Publishing,
an imprint of JMD Media Ltd

ISBN 978-1-78091-395-7

Contents

Testimonial

'Kevin Beattie walks on water.'

Those were the words that my sister Karen and I scrawled, six feet high, in the golden sands of Carbis Bay in Cornwall one bitingly cold April day in the early 1970s. Without wishing to be blasphemous, there were times in those heady days when you could almost bring yourself to believe that message.

Beattie, and the rest of Town's heroes, were just embarking on a decade of almost unbroken success – 10 years in which they brought home the FA Cup, and the UEFA Cup, and challenged for the League Championship season after season, playing exciting, goal-fuelled football.

It was a truly remarkable story. After being promoted back to Division One in 1968, Ipswich had struggled. The first few seasons back in the big-time saw a perpetual battle against relegation. But Bobby Robson managed to transform a team of strugglers into a real force.

The turning point, in my opinion, came in September 1971, and it should serve as an object lesson to all impatient football club chairmen. On the evening of Tuesday 7 September 1971 Manchester United came to Portman Road for a second-round League Cup tie. They played Town off the park, winning 3–1. George Best was particularly inspired that night, scoring twice. Uncharacteristically for the usually patient Ipswich fans, the mood on the terraces turned ugly. There were widespread calls for Robson to be sacked.

The story goes that, having suffered the same fate at Fulham, a dispirited Robson went home that night and told his wife Elsie to start packing, as he fully expected to be sacked the next morning. Instead, club chairman John Cobbold apologised to his manager for the fans' behaviour, and a few days later gave Robson the funds to buy Allan Hunter from Blackburn Rovers. I am utterly convinced that if Cobbold had not been brave enough to stand by his man then the history of Ipswich Town Football Club would have been very different. The glory years which feature in this book might never have happened without Robson at the helm.

The rest, as they say, is history. Hunter became a key part of Robson's building programme and the following season was joined in Town's defence by the prodigiously talented youngster Beattie. From 1972–73 onwards, for the rest of the decade, Town only once finished outside the top six of Division One – and that was the season they won the FA Cup!

Robson's management was masterful. He continually refreshed and strengthened the team. The largely unknown Everton striker David Johnson arrived and a few years later was replaced by the superb Paul Mariner – another hugely important signing. Young, home-grown players burst through: as well as Beattie, there was Brian Talbot, Trevor Whymark, Clive Woods, John Wark – the list goes on and on. Towards the end of the decade, another masterstroke from Robson – the arrival of the Dutch duo, Arnold Muhren and Frans Thijssen. They took Town to a new level.

The undoubted highlight, of course, was that glorious day at Wembley in May 1978, when local boy Roger Osborne won the FA Cup for Town. It was surely written in the stars that Osborne, who hardly ever scored, should be the player to fire home the most famous goal in the club's history.

I hope this book, through more than 300 photographs, captures the true spirit of those thrilling days. The book is dedicated to the players who made the 1970s the most exciting decade for Town fans and, of course, to the manager, Bobby Robson.

Terry Hunt
Ipswich Town fan since 1968.

Foreword

A glorious decade

I was privileged to be the captain of Ipswich Town Football Club for the vast majority of the 1970s, the decade which is featured in this book. It was a time of sustained success for the football club, as Bobby Robson built a team which from 1972–73 until the end of the 1970s only once finished outside the top six of Division One – and that was the year we won the FA Cup!

At the start of the decade, we were struggling to retain our place in the top flight of English football, but some inspired signings plus the emergence of talented youngsters through the youth system transformed us from relegation battlers into one of the best teams in the country.

The arrival of Allan Hunter in 1971 – just a few days after the Portman Road crowd had been calling for Mr Robson's head – was crucial, as was the emergence of brilliant young players like Kevin Beattie, George Burley, Brian Talbot and Trevor Whymark. Our first success was winning the Texaco Cup in 1973. It wasn't the most glamorous of trophies, but it was silverware nonetheless, and the fact that it was Norwich who we beat in the Final was a real bonus!

After losing in heartbreaking and controversial circumstances in the FA Cup semi-final against West Ham in 1975, we were determined not to become the 'nearly men' of English football. That's why winning the FA Cup against Arsenal in 1978 was so extra special for us. That sunny, humid day at the old Wembley Stadium was a fantastic occasion for all of us – players, management, and, of course, the brilliant Ipswich fans. For me, as the man lucky enough to lift the famous trophy, it is a memory which will live with me for ever.

By now, the team included players like John Wark and Paul Mariner, and after our Wembley triumph Mr Robson went about strengthening the line-up again. Most significantly, he signed the brilliant Dutch midfield duo Arnold Muhren and Frans Thijssen. Nowadays, when all the top Premier League teams have a complement of overseas players, it's easy to forget how groundbreaking these signings were back in the late 1970s. Their arrival paved the way for more success, culminating in us winning the UEFA Cup in 1981 and coming agonisingly close to capturing a unique treble. But that's all for a future book.

In hundreds of pictures, this book captures the essence of Ipswich Town's success in the 1970s: the FA Cup roller coaster, the European adventures and, of course, the many memorable games in Division One.

I was lucky enough to have been at the heart of it all. I hope you enjoy the memories.

Mick Mills MBE

Mick Mills was captain of Ipswich Town from 1971 until 1982. He was skipper of the side that won the FA Cup in 1978 and the UEFA Cup in 1981. Mills made 741 appearances for the club, a record which is unlikely ever to be broken.

He also played for England 42 times, and captained his country in the 1982 World Cup Finals. He is now the Suffolk ambassador for the Sir Bobby Robson Foundation, which raises money for cancer research.

1969–70: Signings save the day

In early 1970 it looked for all the world as though Ipswich Town were heading back to Division Two.

A severe lack of goals was the main problem. Town averaged less than a goal a game in the League, and Colin Viljoen ended up as top scorer with a paltry six. Between the beginning of December and mid-March, Ipswich managed only one win in 13 games, and it seemed as though the writing was on the wall.

It was then that Bobby Robson pulled off a masterstroke. He signed winger Jimmy Robertson from Arsenal and striker Frank Clarke from Queen's Park Rangers, and Town recorded four wins and a draw in the last seven games of the season to save themselves. Robertson and Clarke contributed five goals in that run.

Division One final position: 18th

FA Cup: Third round

League Cup: Third round

Manchester United 'keeper Alex Stepney takes the ball off the foot of Town striker Mick Hill in this picture from an FA Cup tie in January 1970. Town lost this third-round game thanks to an own-goal from Mick McNeil. Although Manchester United were a fading force at this point, they still boasted Messrs Charlton and Best in their line-up.

At the beginning of 1970 it looked as though Ipswich Town would be returning to the Second Division after only two seasons back in the big-time. The problem was the team had no goals in it – midfielder Colin Viljoen finished the season as top scorer with a measly six. This picture shows action from the 1–0 home defeat against Burnley in January 1970. Town skipper Bill Baxter is doing his best to put Burnley 'keeper Peter Mellor under pressure. This came during a desperate run of 13 League games in which Town won only once and drew three others. The trapdoor was opening, until the arrival of Jimmy Robertson and Frank Clarke in March energised the team, and they survived.

Defender Mick McNeil clears during Town's 2–0 defeat against Wolves at Molineux in January 1970, a result which increased relegation fears. England international McNeil had joined Town from Middlesbrough in 1964, but after the first two seasons he never really commanded a regular first-team place. He later became well known for running a string of sports shops in East Anglia.

Have boots, will score goals. Frank Clarke signed for Town from Queen's Park Rangers in March 1970, at the same time as Ipswich captured Jimmy Robertson from Arsenal. The two signings proved crucial in a successful relegation fight.

Bill Baxter and David Best combine to snuff out a West Ham attack in a goalless draw at Upton Park in March 1970. The point was precious for Town.

Ipswich Town v Sunderland, 21 March 1970. A real red-letter day in Town's history. Both teams were desperately fighting against relegation. The match marked the debuts of Town's new signings Jimmy Robertson and Frank Clarke, and they inspired Ipswich to a hugely significant 2–0 win, their first in 10 desperate games. The game also marked Trevor Whymark's first goal for the club. An own-goal from visiting defender Richie Pitt also helped Town, who ended the season clear of trouble. Sunderland went down. In the picture, Mick Mills is seen challenging Sunderland 'keeper Derek Forster, who five years earlier had become the club's youngest-ever first-team player, aged just 15.

One of the crucial results which secured Town's place in Division One at the end of the 1969–70 season was a 2–1 home win over Arsenal at the end of March. Bill Baxter and new signing Frank Clarke were Town's scorers. Here, Derek Jefferson is putting Gunners 'keeper Bob Wilson under extreme pressure.

Frank Clarke celebrates one of Town's goals in a 2–0 win over Southampton in April 1970. This was not Clarke's goal, though – his fellow new signing, Jimmy Roberston, was the scorer.

Tommy Carroll sends Southampton 'keeper Eric Martin the wrong way as Town beat the Saints 2–0 in a crucial relegation battle in April 1970.

Town fans celebrate as their heroes continue their great escape from relegation at the end of the 1969–70 season. This picture is from the win against Southampton in April 1970, which Town won 2–0, with goals from new hero Jimmy Robertson and a Tommy Carroll penalty. Ipswich finished five points clear of the drop, thanks to four wins in their last seven games. New signings Jimmy Robertson and Frank Clarke played a huge part.

Town skipper Bill Baxter looks justifiably pleased with himself after the crucial home win over relegation rivals Southampton in April 1970. Colin Harper seems to be more worried about the state of his hair!

Bill Baxter runs on to the pitch for his benefit game in April 1970. As part of the proceedings, an Ipswich Town Past XI took on an Ipswich Town Future XI, which explains why former greats Ted Phillips, Ken Malcolm and Jimmy Leadbetter are joining proceedings. As part of Alf Ramsey's 1962 League Championship-winning side, and a stalwart for the best part of a decade afterwards, Bill Baxter is a true Town legend. But he and Bobby Robson never saw eye to eye, and less than a year after this benefit game Baxter was on his way out of Portman Road in disgrace. He told a national newspaper that the club was 'going to the dogs', was subsequently dropped and was then involved in a punch-up with Robson in the dressing rooms. It was a sad way for such an illustrious Town career to end.

A youthful Brian Talbot is the skipper of the Ipswich Town Future XI as his team prepares to take on the Ipswich Town Past XI as part of Bill Baxter's Testimonial in April 1970.

The Town squad prepares to leave for Zambia at the end of the 1969–70 season. Let us hope they were not planning to make the whole journey in that bus.

1970–71: The struggle goes on

Bobby Robson's second full season at Portman Road was another grim affair. Town once again struggled for goals, managing only one a game in the League. Colin Viljoen was top scorer again, with a paltry 10 in the League. Ipswich finished fourth from bottom, seven points clear of the relegation zone. The FA Cup provided more excitement, with Town seeing off Newcastle and West Bromwich Albion on their way to the fifth round, before going down to Stoke in a replay at Portman Road.

This season marked the end of an era. Long-serving skipper Bill Baxter, the last survivor of Alf Ramsey's League champions, left for Hull City after a very public falling-out with manager Robson. It was an unhappy departure for such a fantastic servant.

Mick Mills, at just 22, became Town's club captain. The first pieces of the jigsaw were being put in place…

Division One final position: 19th

FA Cup: Fifth round

League Cup: Second round

Jimmy Robertson in typical action for Town. His arrival from Arsenal in March 1970 was crucial as Town stayed up. Although he did not stay too long, Robertson was an important capture for Ipswich. He was a huge favourite with the Portman Road faithful. Behind Robertson are Bill Baxter and Tommy Carroll. It would not be long before the pair fell out with Bobby Robson in spectacular fashion.

A goalless draw at Stoke's Victoria Ground was not a bad result on the opening day of the 1970–71 season. Unfortunately, Town could not hit a barn door from five paces in the early part of the campaign, failing to score in any of their first five League games. Here, skipper Bill Baxter is pictured in an aerial battle with Stoke striker John Ritchie.

Town's home game against Nottingham Forest in August 1970 also saw them fire blanks in a goalless draw. Here, Forest 'keeper Peter Barron has the situation under control, despite the attentions of Town striker Frank Clarke.

Saints hardman defender John McGrath puts his foot through the ball as Southampton battle to a 1–0 win over Ipswich at The Dell in the early weeks of the 1970–71 season. Blues skipper Bill Baxter does his best to put McGrath under pressure.

The giant Watneys advert dates this just a little! This is action from Town's 1–0 defeat at Southampton in August 1970. Trevor Whymark does his best to get his head to the ball.

A win at last! At the seventh attempt, Town notched their first League win of the season, 3–0 against Burnley at Portman Road. Bill Baxter, Frank Clarke, and Colin Viljoen (penalty) were on target. Here, Viljoen challenges Burnley 'keeper Tony Waiters in the air.

Clive Woods tries his luck during Town's much-needed 3–0 win over Burnley at Portman Road in August 1970. This was a brief early flourish in Norfolk boy Woods's career. He faded from the first team in the next few seasons, and it was not until the mid-1970s that he re-established himself, having been converted from midfield to left-wing.

That's more like it! After a decidedly dodgy start to the season, Town well and truly hit form when mighty Manchester United came to Portman Road in September 1970. Ipswich beat their illustrious visitors – boasting luminaries such as Best, Law and Charlton – 4–0, with two goals from Colin Viljoen, and one each from Trevor Whymark and Frank Clarke. Here, Clarke celebrates as stand-in 'keeper Jimmy Rimmer is beaten yet again. World Cup-winner Nobby Stiles (number seven) is less amused.

Town players celebrating one of their four goals against Manchester United at Portman Road in September 1970. From left, Trevor Whymark, Clive Woods, Frank Clarke (partially obscured), Mick McNeil, and Jimmy Robertson.

A very young Bobby Robson is keeping his cool in this game at Chelsea in September 1970 – but he should have been spitting feathers. Because this was the match of the infamous 'goal that never was'. Chelsea midfielder Alan Hudson shot wide, the ball rebounding from a stanchion. Town 'keeper David Best collected the ball, and both teams waited for play to restart with a goal-kick. Until, that is, they noticed that referee Roy Capey was signalling for a goal! The bizarre 'goal' put Chelsea two up and, although Frank Clarke pulled one back for Town, they lost 2–1 in the cruellest of circumstances.

Irish full-back Tommy Carroll in action for Ipswich against West Bromwich Albion in October 1970. Carroll had played an important part in Town's promotion season in 1967–68 but had a massive fall-out with manager Bobby Robson during this season and was soon heading for the exit door.

The old 'chicken run' at Portman Road was in its last season in 1970–71. Here, West Bromwich Albion defender John Talbut makes an acrobatic clearance, watched by teammate John Kaye and young Town striker Trevor Whymark. Later in the game, Whymark switched roles, replacing the injured David Best in goal. The game ended 2–2, with Colin Viljoen and Frank Clarke on target.

A terrific goal from Mick Hill saw off visitors Liverpool in October 1970 – a notable scalp for struggling Town. Here, Bill Baxter and Alec Lindsay are having their own sprint competition, with Geoff Hammond trailing behind.

Town defenders Bill Baxter and Geoff Hammond combine to keep out West Ham striker Clyde Best in the game at Portman Road in November 1970. Goals from Mick Hill and Mick Mills saw Town clinch a 2–1 win.

A trip to Elland Road was not something to look forward to in the early 1970s. But Town came away from this game in December 1970 with a creditable point after a battling 0–0 draw. Here it is panic stations in the Town defence as they keep out the Leeds attack, including Allan 'sniffer' Clarke (far right).

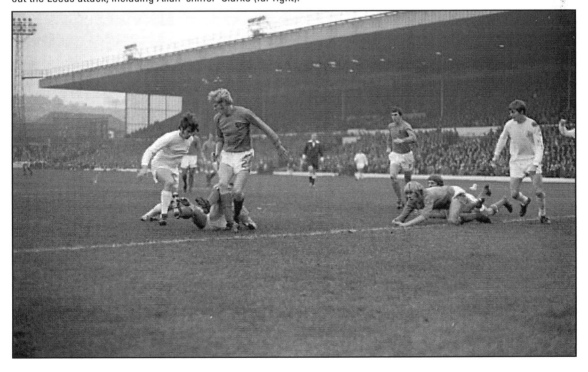

Town enjoyed a rare FA Cup run in 1970–71, reaching the fifth round. This is action from the third round replay against Newcastle at Portman Road, which Ipswich won 2–1 thanks to goals from Colin Viljoen and Mick Hill. Here, Bill Baxter challenges for the ball, watched by a gaggle of players. Among them is the Newcastle 'keeper, whose surname is McFaul. His christian name? Well, that is interesting. Back in the 1970s, he was called Ian, but later on his name changed to Willie. Why? Answers on a postcard…

More action from the FA Cup third round replay against Newcastle in January 1971. Town defender Mick McNeil – later better known for his chain of sports shops – puts Magpies 'keeper McFaul under pressure.

'Warhorse' is one of the words which has been used so often in football reports that it has become a cliché. But that is the only appropriate word to describe Dave Mackay. The hardman Scot had been part of Tottenham's great side in the early 1960s and had a second lease of life when Brian Clough signed him for Derby. Here he is, terrifying Town's Welsh international striker Mick Hill. Town lost this game 1–0 at Portman Road in January 1971.

I am not too sure I would fancy perching in the rather rickety camera gantry! Colin Viljoen tries his luck in the 1–0 defeat against Derby at Portman Road in January 1971. Mick Hill is the other Town player, pitting his wits against Derby defenders John Robson and Terry Hennessy.

The player heading powerfully clear for Blackpool at Portman Road in January 1971 is none other than the legendary Jimmy Armfield. Sadly for Armfield and his teammates, they lost 2–1 to goals from Geoff Hammond (one of only two he scored for Town) and Mick Lambert. Blackpool were relegated at the end of the season.

Arsenal were on their way to an historic League and Cup double when Ipswich visited Highbury in February 1971. Town were on the wrong end of a first-half Blitz, trudging back to the changing rooms 3–0 down at half-time. Two goals from ex-Gunner Jimmy Robertson in the second half made the scoreline more respectable. In the picture, Charlie George puts Town's flying 'keeper Laurie Sivell under pressure.

Here is Frank Lampard playing against Ipswich. Apologies to younger readers – we are not talking about THAT Frank Lampard. No, this is his dad, Frank Lampard Senior, wearing the number-three shirt for West Ham against Town at Upton Park in March 1971. As well as Ronnie Boyce, who is pictured challenging Clive Woods, Lampard had some illustrious teammates that day, including Bobby Moore, Geoff Hurst, and Jimmy Greaves. Greavsie might have been getting on a bit by now, but he still knew the way to goal, as he showed by scoring both Hammers' goals in this 2–2 draw. Town's scorers were defender Bobby Bell and Jimmy Robertson.

Frank Clarke challenges West Ham 'keeper Bobby Ferguson in this 2–2 draw at Upton Park in March 1971. A decent result for inconsistent Town, who by now were being captained by the youthful Mick Mills after Bill Baxter's headline-grabbing fall from grace.

Who says wingers do not get stuck in? Jimmy Robertson getting his shorts dirty as Town grab a 2–2 draw at West Ham in March 1971.

Jimmy Robertson was never short of a word or two of advice for the men in the middle. Here, he looks like he might have got himself into trouble during the 2–2 draw against West Ham at Upton Park in March 1971.

'Keeper's ball! The main problem for Spurs 'keeper Pat Jennings here is the presence of his own teammate Allan Gilzean. Town lost 2–0 in this game at White Hart Lane in April 1971, with England striker Martin Chivers and an own-goal from Peter Morris doing the damage.

Let us be honest – you have to be quite mature to remember when Huddersfield were in the top division! This is evidence that it did happen. Town beat the Terriers 2–0 in April 1971, with Mick Hill and Frank Clarke on target. Huddersfield were relegated the following season, never to return – so far.

The end of an era: the old 'chicken run' is dismantled in May 1971, to be replaced by the brand new East Stand (now the Cobbold Stand) for the new season. Following its removal from Portman Road, the 'chicken run' did loyal service at Foxhall Stadium, home of the Ipswich Witches, until it was unceremoniously wrecked in the hurricane of October 1987.

1971–72: A significant arrival

This was a season of steady, if unspectacular, progress for Ipswich Town. A final position of 13th in the League brought relief from the annual struggle against relegation, with four wins in the last six League games especially welcome. Scoring goals was once again a problem, with Town managing only 39 in their 42 League games.

But the statistics hide the most significant story of the season. On 7 September 1971 Ipswich were annihilated in the League Cup by George Best and Manchester United in front of a highly disgruntled Portman Road crowd. There were widespread calls of 'Robson out' from the terraces.

Instead of sacking his manager, Town chairman John Cobbold apologised to Robson and within days had allowed him to make a highly significant signing – Northern Ireland centre-half Allan Hunter from Blackburn. Hunter's Irish teammate Bryan Hamilton also arrived. Both were to play big roles in the better times which were just around the corner.

Division One final position: 13th

FA Cup: Fourth round

League Cup: Second round

Floodlit action from an historic night at Portman Road. This is the League Cup clash between Town and Manchester United which marked a turning point in Bobby Robson's managerial career. After going ahead through Jimmy Robertson, Town were humiliated by the Reds, and an inspired George Best in particular. The little Irish genius scored twice in a 3–1 win for the Red Devils. The Ipswich fans were less than impressed, and there were widespread chants of 'Robson out' from the terraces. Robson – for whom his dismissal at Fulham was still an unhappy memory – reputedly thought he was on his way again, and told his wife Elsie to start packing. Instead, the next morning, chairman John Cobbold apologised on behalf of the supporters, and a couple of days later allowed his manager to invest money in signing Allan Hunter – a crucial investment. The rest, as they say, is history…

A really significant moment in Town's history. It is 11 September 1971, and Allan Hunter is warming up for his Town debut, against Leicester City at Portman Road. Four days earlier, Town fans had been calling for Bobby Robson's head as George Best destroyed the Blues in the League Cup. The club's response was to invest in Northern Ireland centre-half Hunter to shore up the leaky defence. Although Town lost in his first game, 2–1 to Leicester, Hunter quickly established himself as one of the best players ever to wear the blue shirt. The pieces of the jigsaw were being put into place…

Town's 1971–72 season started very poorly, with only one win in their first eight League games. One of their poor results was a 2-1 home defeat against Leicester City at Portman Road. Frank Clarke scored the Ipswich goal from the spot. In this picture, Mick Hill and Jimmy Robertson try to put the Leicester defence under pressure. The one bright spot of the game was the debut of Allan Hunter.

There is a great view of the new stand at Portman Road during the 1–1 draw against Nottingham Forest in October 1971. Sir Alf Ramsey had officially opened the new stand at the start of the season. Colin Harper was Town's slightly surprising scorer in this game.

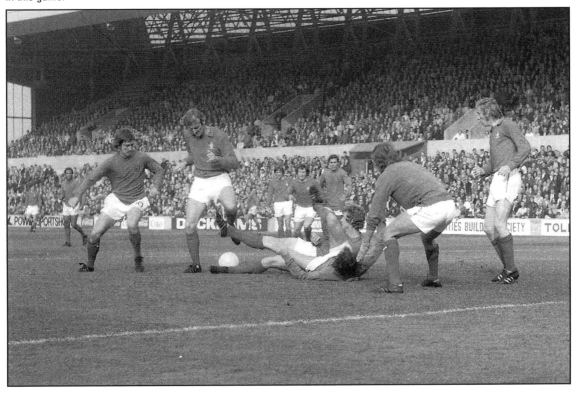

Town and Nottingham Forest fought out a 1–1 draw at Portman Road in October 1971. Here, Mick Hill seems to be winning an aerial battle, while strike partner Frank Clarke looks on. The Ipswich goalscorer in this game was locally born full-back Colin Harper. By coincidence, Forest's scorer was also an Ipswich-born player – Ian Storey-Moore, whose promising career was cut short by injury shortly after he signed for Manchester United in 1974.

Town and Crystal Palace shared the points in this 1–1 draw at Selhurst Park in November 1971, with Mick Hill on target. The Welsh international, seen here in action during the game, ended up as Town's top scorer, albeit with a less-than-impressive eight goals.

Striker Rod Belfitt quickly established himself as a fans' favourite when he signed from Leeds in the autumn of 1971. Here he is, in action in one of his early games for Town against Huddersfield at a snowy Portman Road in November. Mick Hill scored the only goal of the game. The Terriers from Yorkshire were destined for the drop.

Ah, the days when footballers were real men! An arctic scene from Portman Road as Town took on Huddersfield in November 1971.

Ipswich-born winger John Miller is up against experienced Liverpool duo Alec Lindsay (grounded) and Ian Ross in this picture from a game at Portman Road in December 1971. It ended 0–0. A few years later, Miller joined arch-rivals Norwich City and scored twice against Ipswich to knock them out of the League Cup.

Not a Happy New Year for Town fans. On 1 January 1972, Ipswich stormed into a two-goal lead against West Bromwich Albion, through Mick Hill and Rod Belfitt, before letting it slip and crumbling to a 3–2 defeat. In the picture, Hill challenges for the ball in the air.

Action from the Town v West Bromwich Albion game on New Year's Day 1972. After being 2–0 up at half-time, Town conspired to throw it all away and eventually lost 3–2.

Ipswich visited Peterborough in the third round of the FA Cup, coming away with a 2–0 victory thanks to goals from Colin Viljoen and Mick Hill. Here, Viljoen is in charge of matters, and help is at hand from John Miller. Hopes of a Cup run were dashed by a 1–0 defeat at Birmingham in the next round.

Notice the family resemblance? Yes, it's Frank Lampard Senior again, this time trying to stop Jimmy Robertson during Town's 1-0 win over West Ham at Portman Road in January 1972. Also in the thick of the action are Bryan 'Pop' Robson and Colin Viljoen. Peter 'Diesel' Morris scored the all-important goal.

Mick Hill is at full stretch but cannot reach the ball before West Ham 'keeper Peter Grotier. Tommy Taylor looks on during Town's 1–0 win over the visiting Hammers.

There was more FA Cup disappointment for Town in 1971–72. Having overcome Peterborough in the third round, Ipswich were dumped out of the competition by the only goal of the game at Birmingham in the fourth round. Here, winger John Miller and striker Frank Clarke try unsuccessfully to get on the end of a free-kick.

John Miller tries to outwit Birmingham defender Gary Pendrey in the FA Cup defeat in February 1972. This was long-serving defender Mick McNeil's final game for the Blues. Bob Latchford scored the only goal.

Arsenal's all-stars came to Portman Road in February 1972 and left with a 1–0 win thanks to a goal from Charlie George, who had scored the FA Cup Final winner the previous year. In this picture, Rod Belfitt challenges for the ball. Among others featured are Town winger Jimmy Robertson (number seven), playing against his old club, Sammy Nelson (number three) who was to play against Town at Wembley six years later, and England World Cup-winner Alan Ball (far right).

'Big Al' in charge of the situation against Arsenal in February 1972. Hunter was recognised as the best centre-half in the UK. Among his opponents here are Pat Rice and Frank McLintock. Arsenal won this match at Portman Road 1–0.

Careful, 'keeper! Southampton's Eric Martin looks like he is about to do something rash as he challenges Mick Lambert in the 1–1 draw at Portman Road in March 1972. Trevor Whymark was Town's goalscorer.

Rod Belfitt shows his courage by challenging the fearsome Southampton defender John McGrath in the 1–1 draw at Portman Road in March 1972. Belfitt, who had been signed from Leeds, established himself as a real favourite during his short stay at Ipswich.

Colin Viljoen in action against Southampton at Portman Road in March 1972. Waiting to see what develops is young striker Trevor Whymark, who scored Town's goal in a 1–1 draw. Whymark began to establish himself during this season.

Mick Lambert and Rod Belfitt challenge Tottenham 'keeper Pat Jennings in Town's 2–1 win over Spurs at Portman Road in April 1972. Belfitt was one of the Ipswich scorers, with the other being an own-goal from visiting defender Tony Want.

Mick Lambert leads the hapless Huddersfield defence a merry dance in the 3–1 away win towards the end of the 1971–72 season.

The Huddersfield defenders do not like it, but Rod Belfitt has just scored for Ipswich in the away game in April 1972. Peter Morris and Jimmy Robertson were the other scorers for Town in a 3–1 win, which pushed Huddersfield closer to their eventual relegation.

Looking in the record books, Town's 0–0 home draw against Sheffield United in April 1972 looks like a rather dull, uneventful affair. Don't you believe it! This was the game when referee Gordon Kew awarded a controversial penalty for the Blades, Town left-back Colin Harper was sent off – when dismissals were very rare – and furious Town fans responded by throwing plastic seat covers on to the pitch! Fortunately, diminutive Town 'keeper Laurie Sivell managed to save the spot-kick, and 10-man Ipswich held on for a point. This picture shows Town striker Rod Belfitt challenging for the ball. Sheffield's flamboyant midfielder Tony Currie is on the right of the picture.

1972–73: League success – and Cup glory!

This was the start of it all – the first season of what has become known as the Robson glory years. It began with an eye-catching win against Manchester United at Old Trafford, saw Town finish in an impressive fourth place in Division One, qualify for Europe, and the icing on the cake came when Ipswich won the Texaco Cup, against Norwich at Carrow Road of all places. Does it get any better?

This was a breakthrough season for a number of Town youngsters, most notably 18-year-old powerhouse defender Kevin Beattie, who made his debut in the opening day win at Old Trafford, and immediately established himself as a regular. Also significant was the creation of the striking partnership of Trevor Whymark and David Johnson, a signing from Everton in the autumn.

The undoubted highlight was Town's capture of the Texaco Cup. Admittedly it was not English football's most prestigious trophy, but it represented a huge breakthrough for Robson and the club. Ironically, it was Norfolk boys Trevor Whymark and Clive Woods who scored the goals that saw Mick Mills lift the trophy at the home of Norwich City.

Division One final position: Fourth

FA Cup: Fourth round

League Cup: Third round

Texaco Cup: Winners

Ipswich Town's first-team squad for 1972–73. New boy Kevin Beattie has pushed his way to the front! These were the players who began Town's glorious decade as one of English football's finest teams. Bobby Robson, who presided over it all, stands at the back on the far left, looking rather apprehensive. He need not have worried.

After losing at home to Norwich in the first home game of the 1972–73 season, Town bounced back with a 2–0 home win against Birmingham. The goals came from John Miller and Trevor Whymark, who is seen beating former Ipswich full-back Tommy Carroll in the air.

Ipswich fans bask in the early September sunshine as they watch their heroes take on Spurs at Portman Road in 1972. The game ended 1–1, with Colin Viljoen scoring Town's goal.

Legendary 'keeper Pat Jennings thwarts Bryan Hamilton in the game at Portman Road in September 1972.

Colin Viljoen sprays the ball around in a 1–1 draw against West Ham at Portman Road in October 1972. Bryan Hamilton was on target for Town.

Derby 'keeper Colin Boulton looks like he has made a mess of this cross at Portman Road in October 1972. Bryan Hamilton and Rod Belfitt are the Town players closest to the action. Belfitt was one of Town's scorers in a 3–1 win, the others being Kevin Beattie and Trevor Whymark.

Who needs goalline technology? We can all see that Derby defender Terry Hennessey has failed to stop this ball trickling over the line for a Town goal. It looks like Ipswich striker Rod Belfitt is about to tell him as much! This is action from a 3–1 Ipswich win in October 1972. Scorers were Belfitt, Kevin Beattie, and Trevor Whymark.

You are not fooling anyone, Terry – it is a goal. Allan Hunter and Rod Belfitt celebrate as Derby defender Terry Hennessey tries his best to look innocent. Goalmouth action from Town's 3–1 win over Derby in October 1972.

Young Liverpudlian David Johnson is pictured on his Town debut against mighty Leeds United at Portman Road in November 1972. Johnson's arrival from Everton came out of the blue, with Rod Belfitt heading off to Everton. Town held their own in a 2–2 draw, with Trevor Whymark and Paul Madeley (og) the Ipswich scorers.

Ipswich fans leaving the station for the East Anglian derby game at Carrow Road in November 1972. They were not in for a memorable afternoon – the game ended 0–0.

A good action shot of Trevor Whymark playing against Norwich at Carrow Road in November 1972. Norfolk boy Whymark made a habit of scoring important goals against the Canaries, but he drew a blank on this occasion – the game ended goalless.

How was this not a goal? Kevin Beattie has made contact with the ball, and for all the world it looks like it is rocketing into the net past Newcastle 'keeper Ian McFaul. But it was not – because Trevor Whymark, also in the picture, scored the only goal of the game at Portman Road in January 1973.

Young Town stars Kevin Beattie and Trevor Whymark pictured at Ipswich station as they leave for an England Under-23 game in the 1972–73 season. It was on one such trip that 'the Beat' decided it would be a good idea to go home to Carlisle instead of reporting for England duty.

Trevor Whymark might not be in the picture, but the Town striker has just scored the only goal of the game against Newcastle at Portman Road in early January 1973. Bryan Hamilton and the defensive legends Allan Hunter and Kevin Beattie are among those celebrating. On the far right of the picture is the unmistakeable figure of World Cup referee Jack Taylor.

Town were drawn against non-League Chelmsford City in the third round of the FA Cup in 1973. These young fans are pictured at Ipswich station before the relatively short train journey to Chelmsford. Ipswich won 3–0 with goals from Colin Harper, David Johnson and Bryan Hamilton.

A youthful Bobby Robson does well to lift the giant bottle of whisky after being named Bell's Manager of the Month for January 1973. Town were on a roll, with four consecutive wins since Christmas. Bobby was given his award before the home game against Southampton on 27 January. The manager of the month curse did not strike, although Town's winning run did come to an end. They had to settle for a 2–2 draw, with goals from Colin Viljoen and Bryan Hamilton.

How the mighty had fallen. Manchester United were struggling when they visited Ipswich in February 1973, and Town won the game comfortably. Bryan Hamilton scored twice in a 4–1 win, with the other goals coming from Colin Harper and a Colin Viljoen penalty. Here we see Hamilton grabbing one of his goals with 'keeper Alex Stepney helpless on the ground. United finished fifth from bottom in this season and were relegated the following year.

Lightning-quick David Johnson proved a hit with Ipswich fans. Here he is in action against Manchester United at Portman Road in February 1973. Town won 4–1.

Ipswich-born full-back Colin Harper did not score very often, so when he did it was worth celebrating – especially if the goal happened to be against Manchester United! Here, Harper is congratulated by teammates Bryan Hamilton and Trevor Whymark as Town beat their illustrious visitors 4–1. The familar figure in the number-nine shirt, with back to camera, is none other than Bobby Charlton, in his last season with Manchester United.

David Johnson tries his luck against Arsenal at Portman Road in March 1973. The Gunners won this game 2–1, with Trevor Whymark on target for Town. If the crowd looks rather tightly packed, that is because a massive 34,636 people squeezed into the ground that day.

Bryan Hamilton whips in a cross past George 'Geordie' Armstrong during the 2–1 home defeat against Arsenal in March 1973. Overlapping Mick Mills is not needed.

Hunter and Beattie: the best defensive partnership Town have ever had? Here they are, pitting their wits against Manchester City's Francis Lee in April 1973. This was a game at Portman Road, towards the end of Beattie's breakthrough season. It was obvious from day one that Town had unearthed something very, very special. Mick Lambert scored Town's goal in a 1–1 draw against the visitors from Manchester.

It looks like Allan Hunter is badly injured as he is unceremoniously carted off the pitch by a combination of trainer Cyril Lea and players including teammate Bryan Hamilton and Manchester City's Mike Summerbee. Hunter was replaced by Clive Woods in Town's 1–1 home draw with City in April 1973. But Town fans need not have worried – Big Al was back on duty three days later, as Town beat Newcastle United in the Texaco Cup semi-final.

Manchester City centre-half Tommy Booth heads clear during the 1–1 draw at Portman Road in April 1973. Trevor Whymark is grounded, while full-back Colin Harper has ventured a long way forward!

Young Ipswich players showing off the FA Youth Cup in 1973. This triumph added weight to the belief that things really were on the up at Portman Road. Among those pictured are Les Tibbott, Steve Vale, John Stirk, Dale Roberts, Robin Turner, Eric Gates (who seems rather worried about his hair in the rain) and John Peddelty.

David Johnson rides a fearsome-looking tackle from Wolves defender Derek Parkin at Portman Road in April 1973. Town won the game 2–1 with goals from Peter Morris and Trevor Whymark.

Referee Pat Partridge seems to have found something odd about the coin as rival skippers Mick Mills and Duncan Forbes prepare for the toss before the first leg of the Texaco Cup Final at Portman Road in May 1973. Town won the game 2–1, with Peter Morris scoring both, to set up a tense second leg at Carrow Road.

Handbags! Something seems to have riled Canary 'keeper Kevin Keelan during the first leg of the Texaco Cup Final at Portman Road in May 1973. Referee Pat Partridge tries to keep the peace.

Kevin Keelan is disconsolate after being beaten by one of Peter Morris's goals in the first leg of the Texaco Cup Final at Portman Road in May 1973.

With delicious irony, Norfolk-born duo Clive Woods and Trevor Whymark scored the goals in the second leg of the Texaco Cup Final at Carrow Road. Town won the game 2–1 and took the Cup 4–2 on aggregate. Here, Woods slots his goal past helpless 'keeper Kevin Keelan. Whymark is the other Town player, while the Canaries defender is Dave Stringer.

Where does it hurt, Mick? Bobby Robson and Cyril Lea tend to a stricken Mick Lambert during the second leg of the Texaco Cup Final at Carrow Road in May 1973.

Norfolk boy Trevor Whymark is mobbed by teammates after scoring one of Town's goals in the second leg of the Texaco Cup Final against Norwich at Carrow Road in May 1973. Town won 4–2 on aggregate. Kevin Beattie and Ian Collard (number eight) are in the thick of the celebrations, while Town's number nine, who is just about to join the group hug, is Clive Woods, another Norfolk lad who also scored for Town in this game.

The start of something big! OK, it was only the Texaco Cup, but it was significant for two reasons. Firstly, it put the seal on a season in which Town had made enormous leaps forward, finishing fourth in Division One and qualifying for Europe. Secondly, of course, they beat Norwich in a Cup Final at Carrow Road! Here, Mick Mills is all smiles as he lifts the Cup. By contrast, Town chairman John Cobbold is maintaining a stiff upper lip.

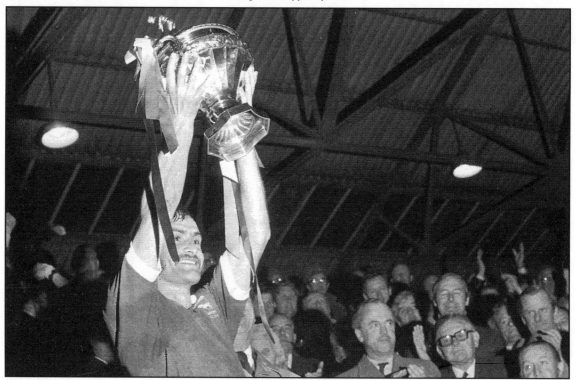

We've won the Cup! Town manager Bobby Robson and coach Cyril Lea celebrate the Texaco Cup victory at Carrow Road in May 1973.

Town fans on the Cornhill in Ipswich after the Texaco Cup triumph.

Skipper Mick Mills shows off the Texaco Cup to the fans from the balcony of Ipswich Town Hall. David Johnson, Kevin Beattie and Ian Collard are enjoying the occasion.

1973–74: European adventure begins

When the draw for the first round of the UEFA Cup was made, Ipswich Town were given the best possible tie: they were playing European legends Real Madrid!

Undaunted, Town saw off their glamorous opponents, thanks to a 1–0 win at Portman Road followed by a gritty goalless draw in the Bernabeu Stadium. Next came Italians Lazio, whose disgraceful tactics in both legs of the tie did them no good as they were dumped out of the tournament. Town then saw off Dutchmen Twente, before losing in a heartbreaking penalty shoot-out to Lokomotiv Leipzig in the quarter-final.

On the domestic front, Town once again finished fourth, with the goalscoring trio of Bryan Hamilton, Trevor Whymark and David Johnson netting more than 50 times between them. The highlight in the League was the 7–0 thrashing of West Brom at Portman Road in February, equalling the club's record victory.

George Burley made his debut, marking George Best in the Manchester United legend's final game at Old Trafford.

Division One final position: Fourth

FA Cup: Fifth round

League Cup: Fourth round

UEFA Cup: Quarter-final

The beginning of a new era – European football returned to Portman Road for the first time in more than a decade in September 1973, with none other than Real Madrid the illustrious visitors in the first round of the UEFA Cup. Town grabbed a notable first-leg victory, winning 1–0 when a Mick Mills shot was deflected into his own net by Spanish defender Rubinan. In the second leg, Town performed heroics in the San Siro, holding out for a 0–0 draw and going through to the next round.

A tense moment from the UEFA Cup first round, first leg against Real Madrid at Portman Road.

Town won this clash with Burnley 3–2 at Portman Road in September 1973, with two goals from Bryan Hamilton and a rare strike from home-grown left-back Colin Harper. In this picture, Mick Lambert is attempting something acrobatic. Burnley's Peter Noble obviously finds it hair-raising!

Legendary hardman Norman 'Bites Yer Legs' Hunter is under pressure from Trevor Whymark in this League Cup tie against Leeds at Portman Road in October 1973. David Johnson and Bryan Hamilton were on target in Town's 2–0 win.

Trevor Whymark and David Webb seem to be on a collision course during this game at Stamford Bridge in October 1973. Whymark was not among the scorers that day, but Town won the game 3–2, thanks to two goals from David Johnson and another from Bryan Hamilton.

He is behind you! Speedy Mick Lambert seems blissfully unaware that the fearsome Ron 'Chopper' Harris is chasing him during Town's 3–2 victory at Stamford Bridge in October 1973.

Chelsea midfielder John Hollins dispossesses Trevor Whymark during the game at Stamford Bridge. Town won the game 3–2.

Otley boy Roger Osborne had been on Town's books for a while before he finally made his first-team debut in 1973–74. Here he is in one of his early games, against Wolves in October 1973. Town won the game 2–0, thanks to goals from Peter Morris and Bryan Hamilton. No one would have guessed that Osborne would become a Town legend.

David Johnson celebrates after scoring one of the goals in Town's 3–0 victory against Coventry at Portman Road in March 1974. Peter Morris and Brian Talbot, who scored Town's two other goals, are among teammates congratulating the Liverpool-born striker.

Brian 'Noddy' Talbot powers through to score for Town in the 3–0 win against Coventry at Portman Road in 1973–74. Local boy Talbot scored his first senior goal in this game, and enjoyed it so much he added another!

Scorer Mick Lambert and David Johnson follow the ball into the net as Town are on their way to a 3–0 home win over Derby in November 1973. 'Keeper Colin Boulton and England centre-half Roy McFarland are not happy. Lambert scored twice in this game, with Kevin Beattie grabbing the other.

Kevin Beattie, who has regularly been named as Ipswich Town's greatest-ever player, shows his power in beating Birmingham centre-half Roger Hynd in the air. This was not a happy occasion for Beattie and his Town teammates, however: they lost this fourth-round League Cup tie 3–1 at Portman Road, with Bob Latchford grabbing a hat-trick.

Town were enjoying their first foray into the UEFA Cup, seeing off Real Madrid, Lazio and then Dutch side Twente Enschede. After a 1–0 home win against Twente, goals from Peter Morris and Bryan Hamilton secured a 2–1 win in Holland, 3–2 on aggregate. The picture shows Hamilton scoring his goal.

Defender Geoff Hammond did not score many goals for Town – so you could forgive him for looking surprised when he did find the back of the net. Here he is celebrating his goal in a 3–0 win against Birmingham just before Christmas in 1973. Mick Lambert scored Town's other goals.

You're having a laugh, ref! Kevin Keelan leads the Canary protests as Ipswich are awarded a penalty at Carrow Road in the Boxing Day derby in 1973. David Johnson seems rather happier. It was Johnson who scored from the spot in a 2–1 Town win.

David Johnson wheels away in triumph, as Kevin Keelan is left in the mud. Johnson has just scored from the penalty spot against Norwich City at Carrow Road on Boxing Day 1973. Mick Lambert added a second Town goal in a 2–1 win. The Canaries were heading for relegation, having escaped by the skin of their teeth the previous season.

'Right, George, you are making your first-team debut today, at Old Trafford, and you are marking George Best.' It couldn't have come much tougher for the 17-year-old Burley a few days after Christmas in 1973. But the youngster acquitted himself well, marking the Irish legend out of the game. It was a shame his more experienced teammates did not perform – Town lost 2–0. It was Best's last game at Old Trafford.

In January 1974, Town skipper Mick Mills notched up his 300th Town appearance. He would, of course, go on to play a record 741 games for the club. It is a record that is very unlikely to be beaten.

David Johnson is about to be congratulated by Mick Mills and Bryan Hamilton after scoring in the 1–1 draw against Stoke City at Portman Road in January 1974.

Geoff Hammond in the treatment room at Portman Road at the beginning of 1974. Local lad Hammond never really established himself as a first-team regular with Ipswich. Being a right-back at a club which also had George Burley and Mick Mills on the books did not help his cause.

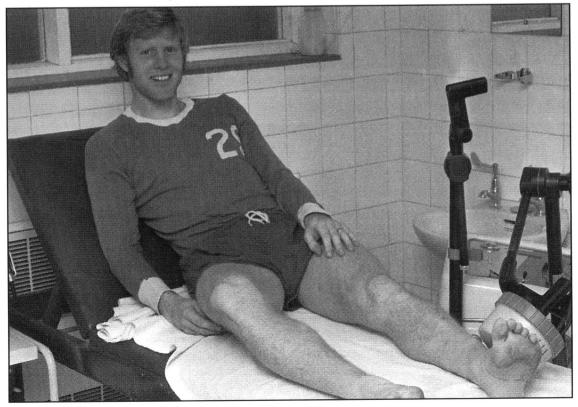

Full-backs united: a boyish George Burley, Colin Harper and Bruce Twamley pictured in 1973–74. Burley made his debut during this season – marking George Best at Old Trafford, no less. For Harper, this season was less memorable – he suffered a serious injury which eventually curtailed his career. Canadian Twamley made the grand total of two appearances for Town.

Town went to Old Trafford in the FA Cup fourth round in January 1974 and came away with a 1–0 win courtesy of Kevin Beattie's goal. Here, Bryan Hamilton celebrates the game's only goal.

Bryan Hamilton was Town's top scorer in 1973–74 season, with a total of 19. Here we see one of his easier finishes, as he scores from about an inch against West Ham at Portman Road in February 1974. 'Keeper Mervyn Day is helpless. Unfortunately, the goal was only a consolation for Town, as the Hammers won the game 3–1, with goals from Mick Mills (og), full-back John McDowell and striker Clyde Best.

Trevor Whymark demonstrates his legendary aerial ability against West Ham at Portman Road in February 1974. His strike partner David Johnson's leap looks rather weedy in comparison. Town lost this game 3–1, which was something of a comedown, as only three days earlier they had thrashed West Bromwich Albion 7–0, with Whymark scoring twice.

Trevor Whymark was Town's goalscorer in the 1–1 draw against Spurs at White Hart Lane in February 1974. Here is Whymark making life uncomfortable for Spurs 'keeper Pat Jennings.

Bryan Hamilton celebrates his goal in a 1–1 draw against Norwich at Portman Road in March 1974. 'Keeper Kevin Keelan and defenders Mel Machin and Dave Stringer (on the ground) look less than pleased. This was not a great result for Town – the Canaries were relegated after finishing rock bottom of Division One.

A smiling Mick Mills proudly leads out the Town side for the UEFA Cup quarter-final against Lokomotiv Leipzig in March 1974. The second leg was to end in heartbreak for Mills and Town, however. The Ipswich skipper was sent off and Ipswich went out on penalties.

Strike partners Trevor Whymark and David Johnson in action during the UEFA Cup quarter-final first leg against Lokomotiv Leipzig at Portman Road in March 1974. Ipswich won the game 1–0 with a goal from Kevin Beattie. But heartbreak was waiting in the second leg.

1973–74 saw the breakthrough of Ipswich boy Brian Talbot, whose non-stop running quickly endeared him to Town fans. Here he is pictured in typically dogged style against Lokomotiv Leipzig in the UEFA Cup quarter-final in March 1974.

Town players sightseeing in Leipzig before their UEFA Cup quarter-final second-leg game in March 1974. Kevin Beattie and Clive Woods lead the way, with Woods sporting a rather stylish leather jacket and matching gloves.

Kevin Beattie scores during the penalty shoot-out at the end of the UEFA Cup tie second leg at Leipzig. Beattie's central defensive partner Allan Hunter – arguably man of the match following the dismissal of Mick Mills – was not so fortunate.

Heartbreak in Germany. Allan Hunter's penalty is saved and Town go out of the UEFA Cup at the quarter-final stage. It was cruel on Hunter, who had performed heroics following the first-half red card for skipper Mick Mills. This unhappy night was 20 March 1974.

1974–75: So near and yet so far

Ipswich Town came so close to glory in 1974–75, but eventually the season ended in heartbreak. In the League, Town moved up a place to third, agonisingly only two points behind League champions Derby County, and with a better goal average.

But the real story was in Town's FA Cup run. The quarter-final against mighty Leeds United turned into a real epic, going to no fewer than three replays. The second and third replays were played just 48 hours apart at Leicester's Filbert Street ground, with a 'banana shot' from winger Clive Woods eventually settling the game in favour of Town.

Injury-hit Ipswich drew 0–0 with West Ham in the semi-final at Villa Park, but it was the replay at Stamford Bridge that has stayed in Town fans' memories, for all the wrong reasons. Ipswich, with teenager John Wark in the patched-up defence, had two 'goals' from Bryan Hamilton controversially disallowed by referee Clive Thomas and lost 2–1. There were tears in the dressing room, and to this day Ipswich players and fans alike are convinced they suffered a huge injustice.

Division One final position: Third
FA Cup: Semi-final
League Cup: Fifth round
UEFA Cup: First round

Oops! Everton 'keeper David Lawson looks like he has let this cross slip, under pressure from Trevor Whymark. Visiting centre-half Roger Kenyon and Bryan Hamilton await developments in this game at Portman Road in September 1974. Clive Woods scored the only goal of the game. Town pipped Everton to third place by a single point.

Mick Lambert was not renowned for his heading skills, but he is soaring way above the Everton defence here, in this game from September 1974. Clive Woods, who is also in the picture, scored the goal in a 1–0 Town win.

Ipswich enjoyed only a short-lived UEFA Cup run in 1974–75. Welcoming Dutch visitors FC Twente to Portman Road, Town were rather too hospitable and allowed them to return to Holland with a 2–2 draw. Brian Talbot, seen being congratulated here, and Bryan Hamilton were Town's goalscorers. Despite another Hamilton goal, the away leg ended 1–1, and Ipswich went out on away goals.

How times change. When Chelsea came to Portman Road in September 1974, they were heading for relegation. Ipswich beat the Londoners 2–0, with goals from Brian Talbot and David Johnson. In this picture, Allan Hunter is throwing his weight around to good effect.

The home League game against Leeds ended goalless. Here, Allan Hunter is adding his goal threat to Town's attack, soaring above Norman Hunter and Terry Yorath. These two sides were to see a lot of each other during this season.

Trevor Whymark tries his luck in a 1–1 home draw against Manchester City in October 1974. Bryan Hamilton was on target for Ipswich, while England midfielder Colin Bell scored for City. Lining up at left-back for the visitors was Willie Donachie, a future Town assistant manager.

Bryan Hamilton, Trevor Whymark and Brian Talbot contest possession with Manchester City's Colin Bell in the Portman Road clash in October 1974. Both Hamilton and Bell were on target that day.

Spot the ball! Liverpool defender Chris Lawler is sandwiched between Brian Talbot and David Johnson as Trevor Whymark and Brian Hall look on. Hall, along with teammate Steve Heighway, created quite a stir as Britain's first 'footballing graduates'. Talbot scored Town's goal in a 1–0 home win against the mighty Reds in November 1974. Liverpool finished second in the League, one place ahead of Town on goal average.

Ipswich beat mighty Liverpool 1–0 with a goal from Brian Talbot at Portman Road in November 1974. Here, Town striker David Johnson, playing against his home-town team, gets between the Liverpool defensive duo of Tommy Smith and Emlyn Hughes.

Kevin Beattie showing his power against Wolves at Molineux in November 1974. The Wolves defenders are Mike Bailey (left) and John McAlle. Town lost this game 2–1, with Clive Woods the scorer.

Wolves 'keeper Phil Parkes punches clear under pressure from Kevin Beattie during Town's 2–1 defeat at Molineux in November 1974.

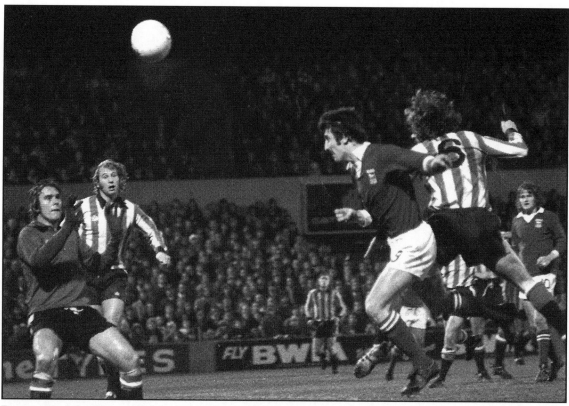

Town reached the fifth round of the League Cup in 1974–75, before Norwich halted their progress. In the fourth round, Ipswich beat Stoke 2–1 at Portman Road, with goals from David Johnson, pictured here, and Bryan Hamilton.

An unhappy night at Carrow Road. Town were enjoying a rare run in the League Cup, and were drawn against old rivals Norwich City in the fifth round. Norwich were in the old second division, so high-flying Town were red-hot favourites. The game at Carrow Road – featured here – ended 1–1, with Norfolk boy Trevor Whymark on target for Town. But the replay ended disastrously for the Suffolk side. Despite David Johnson's goal, it was former Ipswich winger John Miller who scored both goals to send the Canaries chirping all the way back up the A140. Norwich went on to reach the Final, only to lose 1–0 to Aston Villa. This picture shows action from the first leg at Carrow Road, with Allan Hunter heading clear from the Norwich strike duo of Ted MacDougall and Phil Boyer.

Trevor Whymark looks badly injured as he is carried from the pitch against Spurs in December 1974. But the Town striker soon recovered – he completed the whole game as Town romped to a 4–0 win with goals from Colin Viljoen, Kevin Beattie, Mick Lambert and Roger Osborne – his first for Ipswich. In the background, Town manager Bobby Robson chats with substitute Ian Collard.

Boxing Day 1974 proved to be very frustrating for Ipswich Town and their supporters. Relegation-bound Luton Town would surely prove lambs to the slaughter for high-flying Ipswich? Wrong! Town had all the play, but the ball just would not go in. In a rare Luton attack Ron Futcher (one of the blond twins) scored, and Town lost the game 1–0. When you study the final Division One League table, if Town had beaten Luton they would have been champions. Here, Luton 'keeper Graham Horn gratefully drops on the ball as yet another Town attack is snuffed out. Trevor Whymark, Bryan Hamilton and Mick Lambert are the frustrated forwards.

There is no way through, Trevor. Town are on their way to a shock 1–0 home defeat at the hands of struggling Luton on Boxing Day 1974. Here, Trevor Whymark's path to goal is blocked by yet another last-ditch tackle.

Colin Viljoen and Liverpool's Emlyn 'Crazy Horse' Hughes look like they are performing a dance routine during this game at Anfield in February 1975. Town lost the game 5–2, with Kevin Beattie and Trevor Whymark on target. Liverpool and Ipswich finished level on points at the end of the season, but the Merseysiders grabbed the runners'-up spot on goal average, leaving Ipswich third.

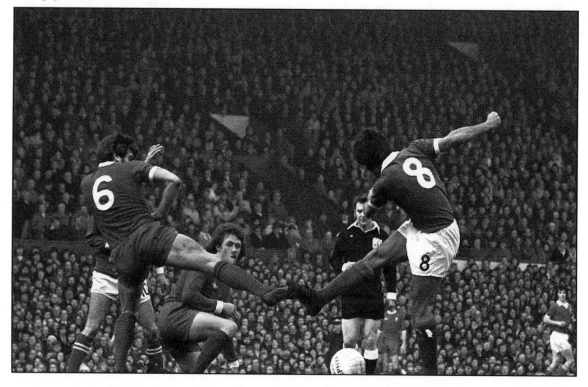

Town's FA Cup fifth-round tie against Aston Villa at Portman Road in February 1975 was an extraordinary affair. Town were 2–0 down and apparently heading out of the tournament before staging a remarkable recovery to win 3–2. David Johnson is seen here scoring Town's first goal. Two strikes from Bryan Hamilton completed the comeback.

Brian Talbot goes round Villa 'keeper Jim Cumbes during Town's remarkable 3–2 win in the FA Cup fifth round at Portman Road in 1975. Seconds later, Bryan Hamilton, the ultimate poacher, had nipped in and Town were on their way to the quarter-final.

Town staged a thrilling comeback against Aston Villa in the fifth round of the FA Cup in February 1975. Ipswich were 2–0 down and seemingly on their way out of the competition. But a goal from David Johnson gave home fans hope, and then Bryan Hamilton replaced Clive Woods and the fireworks really began. The ebullient Irishman scored twice to secure an extraordinary win. Here, Hamilton is being congratulated by teammates David Johnson and Brian Talbot.

There is a right old pile-up in the goalmouth but the main thing is that Town have scored! Ipswich beat Derby 3–0 at Portman Road in February 1975, with goals from Kevin Beattie, David Johnson, and Bryan Hamilton. Both Beattie and Johnson are involved here as Town celebrations begin. Given this easy victory, it was rather ironic that Derby should eventually end up as League champions, two points ahead of Town.

Kevin Beattie is celebrating, Bryan Hamilton is not sure, and David Johnson's facial expression is not visible! These three were the scorers in this 3–0 victory over Derby County at Portman Road in February 1975.

The beginning of a really dramatic saga: Colin Viljoen and Allan Clarke are seen in action in the first meeting of Ipswich and Leeds in the FA Cup sixth round in March 1975. The tie would eventually take four games to settle – in Town's favour. This instalment ended goalless. This game attracted 38,010 fans, still a Portman Road record.

Clive Woods tussles for the ball with Everton defender John Hurst at Goodison Park in March 1975. The game ended 1–1, with Trevor Whymark scoring Town's goal.

Is Big Al's pipe a joke? Town players are in good spirits as they leave by coach to take on Leeds in one of the epic FA Cup quarter-final replays at Leicester in March 1975. The players pictured are: Kevin Beattie, Eric Gates, Paul Cooper, Laurie Sivell, Clive Woods, Roger Osborne and (seated) Allan Hunter and a rather amused Colin Viljoen.

Filbert Street, Leicester, on the evening of Thursday 27 March 1975. Ipswich Town and Leeds United are contesting their FA Cup quarter-final for the fourth time in a matter of 19 days. This is the third replay, coming only two days after the second replay at the same venue finished goalless. This one was a classic. Trevor Whymark put Town ahead, as shown here, before Allan 'sniffer' Clarke levelled things. A lucky Bryan Hamilton deflection put Ipswich back in front, only for Johnny Giles to level things up again. It took a wonderful, swerving 'banana shot' from Clive Woods to clinch things and send Town to their first FA Cup semi-final. John Wark, a raw 17-year-old, who made his debut in this game, can be glimpsed on the right of the picture.

The fixtures were piling up, and injuries were starting to hit Town hard when they hosted Birmingham in a League game on April Fool's Day 1975. A makeshift Town side still managed to come out on top 3–2, with Ian Collard scoring on a rare appearance. The other scorers were Clive Woods, seen celebrating in the number-nine shirt in the absence of the injured David Johnson, and Mick Lambert. During an incredible 11-day spell, Town had to play six games, including two FA Cup quarter-final replays – and they did not lose any of them.

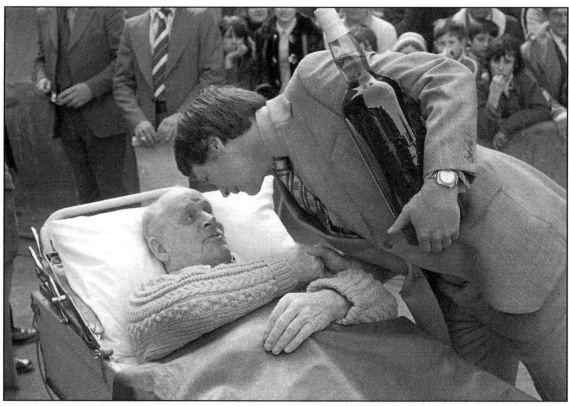

To the end of his life, Bobby Robson always found time for the fans. Here he is, chatting to a Town supporter after being presented with the award as Bell's Manager of the Month in April 1975.

Alan Taylor is held aloft by ecstatic West Ham teammates after scoring in the FA Cup semi-final replay at Stamford Bridge. Taylor scored twice as Town went down to a controversial 2–1 defeat. A grounded Kevin Beattie gives young teammate John Wark (number five) a rueful look. It was teenager Wark's mistake which had led to the goal.

It is the evening of 9 April 1975, a cold and sometimes snowy night at Stamford Bridge. Referee Clive Thomas certainly did nothing to warm these frozen-looking Town fans during the semi-final replay against West Ham.

The man in the middle of controversy during Town's FA Cup semi-final replay against West Ham in 1975. Referee Clive Thomas disallowed two Bryan Hamilton 'goals' and the Hammers went on to win 2–1, with both goals being scored by Alan Taylor – who then went on to grab another two in the Cup Final against Fulham, Bobby Moore and all. In this picture, Mr Thomas is laying down the law to Hammers 'keeper Mervyn Day.

West Ham striker Billy Jennings has just sliced Mick Lambert's corner into his own net, and Town are back on level terms in the FA Cup semi-final replay at Stamford Bridge in April 1975. But the night would end in tears.

A disconsolate John Wark leaves the pitch at Stamford Bridge after Town's controversial and heartbreaking FA Cup semi-final defeat against West Ham in April 1975. The teenage Wark, playing one of his first games for Ipswich, made a mistake for one of Alan Taylor's two goals. But Warky would enjoy many, many better days in a Town shirt – and he certainly was not the villain of the piece on that cold, snowy night in west London!

A disconsolate Trevor Whymark leaves the pitch after Town's defeat in the FA Cup semi-final replay. Unlike many of his teammates that evening, Whymark was never to play in an FA Cup Final – injury robbed him of his chance three years later.

Even the ever-bubbly Kevin Beattie looks downbeat as he shakes Graham Paddon's hand after Town's cruel FA Cup semi-final defeat against West Ham in 1975. Three years later, Beattie's Cup experience was a rather happier one.

1975–76: Season of change

This was a transitional campaign for Town, as Bobby Robson shuffled the pack. Bryan Hamilton departed for Everton, and David Johnson's goals dried up in his final season for Town. This left only Trevor Whymark making a significant contribution in the goalscoring column. As a result, Town's League performances suffered, and they dropped to sixth place, missing out on qualifying for Europe.

Neither the FA Cup nor the League Cup provided much excitement for Town fans, and hopes of a run in the UEFA Cup were dashed with a shocking 4–0 defeat in the away leg at FC Bruges, after Ipswich had established an apparently commanding 3–0 lead in the first leg at Portman Road.

Sadly, this was the season in which Kevin Beattie started to suffer from serious injury problems.

Division One final position: Sixth

FA Cup: Fourth round

League Cup: Second round

UEFA Cup: Second round

Appearances can be deceptive: for all the world, this looks like a rampaging Trevor Whymark scoring against yet another hapless 'keeper. But in fact, Whymark was thwarted by Newcastle 'keeper Mike Mahoney and Town were thumped 3–0 by the Geordie visitors in this opening League game of the season at Portman Road in August 1975. Town failed to win any of their first four League games.

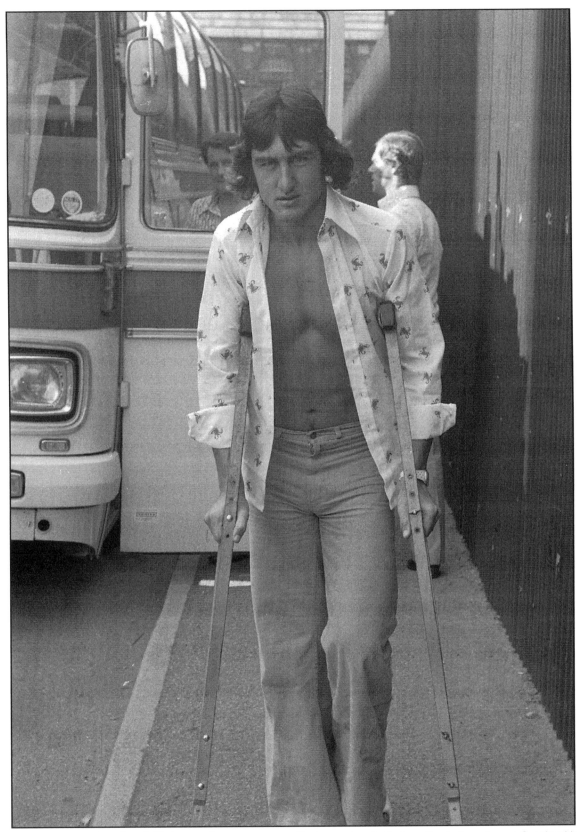

Brian Talbot looks less than thrilled to see the cameraman as the team return to Portman Road after a League Cup tie with Leeds in September 1975. You cannot blame him, really: Town lost the game 3–2, and Talbot suffered a broken leg. In the background are Bobby Robson and physio Brian Simpson.

Bobby Robson does not look too impressed as Town take on Spurs at White Hart Lane in August 1975. Colin Viljoen scored Town's goal in a 1–1 draw. Ipswich made a disappointing start to the season, winning only three of their opening 11 games. They recovered to finish sixth in the First Division. Alongside Robson is coach Cyril Lea and a youthful Eric Gates.

Happy Town fans leaving Felixstowe for the UEFA Cup away leg against Feyenoord in September 1975. They would return in a good mood as well, because Town's 2–1 away victory set them up for a 4–1 aggregate win.

On a filthy September 1975 night in Rotterdam, Town put in a masterful display to see off Dutch giants Feyenoord 2–1, and went on to win this UEFA Cup first-round tie 4–1 on aggregate. The goals on the night came from Clive Woods and Trevor Whymark. Here, the complete Town back four is seen in action, with George Burley on the ball and assistance from Mick Mills, Kevin Beattie and Allan Hunter available. Was this Town's best-ever defence?

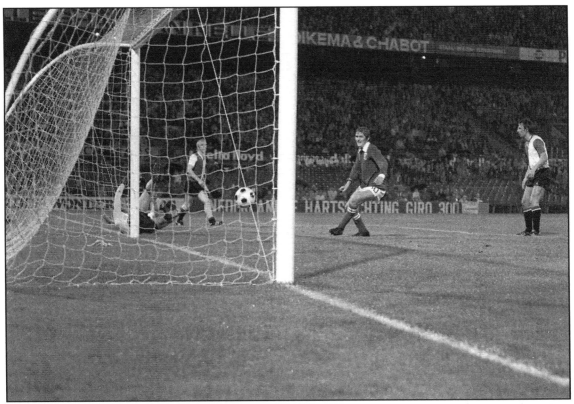

Trevor Whymark nets the second Ipswich goal in a 2–1 UEFA Cup first-leg victory in Rotterdam in September 1975. Town won the second leg 2–0.

It is celebration time at Portman Road as Bryan Hamilton's goal seals victory over arch-rivals Norwich City in September 1975. Town beat the Canaries 2–0, with the other goal coming from Kevin Beattie, also seen joining in the celebrations.

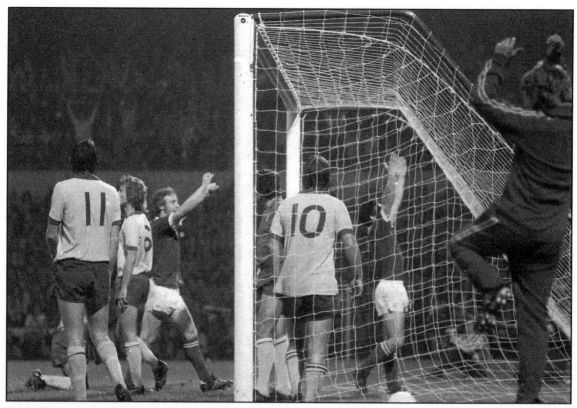

The ballboy cannot resist joining in the celebrations as Bryan Hamilton scores Town's second goal in a 2–0 win over Norwich at Portman Road in September 1975. Kevin Beattie – just about to congratulate Hamilton – was the other Ipswich scorer.

Feyenoord 'keeper Eddy Treytel's comb-over is in serious danger of being disturbed by a leaping Trevor Whymark during Town's 2–0 win in the UEFA Cup first round, second leg against Feyenoord at Portman Road in October 1975. Whymark and strike partner David Johnson scored the Ipswich goals to secure a 4–1 aggregate victory.

Eric Gates blasts the ball home for his first Town goal. This put Ipswich on their way to a 3–0 win over Bruges in the UEFA Cup first round, first leg at Portman Road in October 1975.

Skipper Mick Mills played his 400th game for Ipswich in November 1975. Here he marks the occasion with club stalwart Tommy Parker, whose club appearances record he would go on to break.

The smile was soon to be well and truly wiped from Mick Mills's face! The captains shake hands before the away leg of the UEFA Cup first-round tie against Bruges in 1975. Town led 3–0 from the home leg. Surely they could not throw it away? They did.

A torrid night in Belgium. Ipswich had comfortably won the home leg of this UEFA Cup second-round tie in 1975. They headed to Bruges with a commanding 3–0 lead. But the Belgians stunned Town and their army of fans by turning things round, winning 4–0 on the night, and dumping Town out of the competition. Here, the Ipswich defence struggles to keep the rampant home forwards at bay.

Action from a goalless draw at Filbert Street in November 1975. Town were to finish one place and one point ahead of Leicester in 1975–76. Here, Mick Mills, John Peddelty and Roger Osborne contest possession with Steve Kember and Chris Garland (number nine).

A murky afternoon at Portman Road in November 1975, and Ipswich are heading for one of their 14 League draws of the season. Trevor Whymark was Town's scorer against Sheffield United. Here, Roger Osborne and Mick Lambert battle for possession.

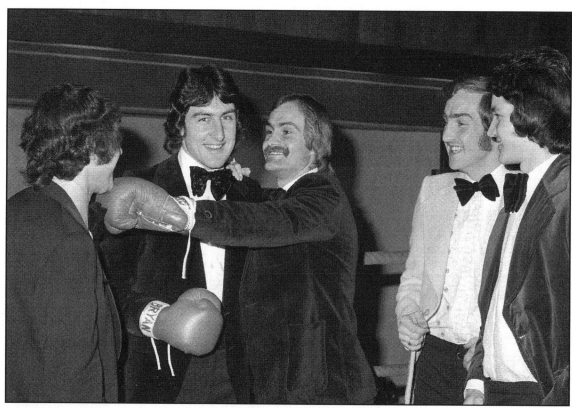

Probably just as well you stuck to football, Mick! Town skipper Mills lands a playful punch during his testimonial dinner in 1975–76. Brian Talbot, John Peddelty and George Burley are the amused onlookers.

Arsenal 'keeper Jimmy Rimmer frustrates Kevin Beattie and Trevor Whymark this time, but he was unable to prevent Clive Woods and Allan Hunter scoring for Town in a 2–0 Boxing Day win at Portman Road in 1975.

Simple pleasures! Town players enjoying a cuppa after a training session in January 1976. From left are Eric Gates, Allan Hunter (who looks like someone has taken his sugar!), David Johnson, Brian Talbot, Mick Lambert, Terry Austin, a rather downbeat-looking George Burley and Kevin Beattie.

Halifax Town were no match for Ipswich in the third round of the FA Cup in 1976, Town winning 3–1 with a Mick Lambert hat-trick. One of his goals is shown here.

Mick Lambert and Trevor Whymark are about to demonstrate an early example of the 'high-five' as the winger celebrates one of his three goals against Halifax in the third round of the FA Cup in 1976.

Nice Y-fronts, lads! Town players pictured in the changing room after a 1–1 home draw against Coventry in January 1976. From left, Allan Hunter – complete with post-match cigarette – Kevin Beattie, Bryan Hamilton, Colin Viljoen, David Johnson and Trevor Whymark. Roger Osborne was Town's goalscorer.

David Johnson and Roger Osborne are thwarted by Coventry 'keeper Jim Blyth in this game at Portman Road in January 1976; however, local lad Osborne did score Town's goal in this 1–1 draw.

Skipper and stalwart Mick Mills was granted a well-deserved testimonial in 1975–76. Here he is, pulling the raffle tickets out of a box at his testimonial dance.

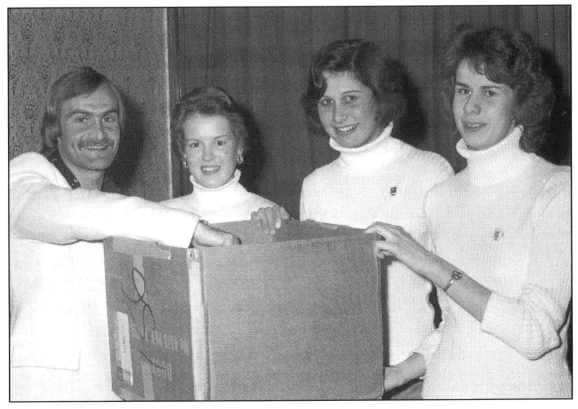

David Johnson might be struggling to win the ball here, but he was on target for Town in this 2–1 win against Sheffield United at Bramall Lane in March 1976. Mick Mills scored a rare goal that afternoon.

Coach Cyril Lea and a youthful Russell Osman help a stricken Mick Lambert from the pitch during Town's 2–1 home win over Manchester City in April 1976. Despite appearances, however, Lambert had a good night, scoring one of Town's goals, with the other coming from Trevor Whymark.

Ugly scenes as Manchester United fans go on the rampage at Portman Road in April 1976. This was arguably the worst example of crowd violence seen at Portman Road. Town won the game 3–0, with goals from Mick Lambert, Trevor Whymark and David Johnson. It was Johnson's last goal for Town. He returned to Merseyside at the end of the season, signing for Liverpool.

Mick Mills looks less composed than usual during this home game against Derby County at Portman Road, the last match of the 1975–76 season. It is not surprising, really, as Derby thumped Town 6–2, with two goals apiece from Francis Lee, Kevin Hector and Bruce Rioch. Mick Lambert and Trevor Whymark replied for the home side.

Brian Talbot's 1975–76 season was badly disrupted by a broken leg, meaning he played in fewer than half of the League games. So, he was still full of energy as the campaign came to an end. Here he is, having a shot on goal during Town's last match of the season, a dismal 6–2 home defeat to Derby.

1976–77: Mariner arrives

After a three-way transfer tussle involving West Ham and West Brom, Bobby Robson landed highly rated Plymouth striker Paul Mariner in October. In only Mariner's second game, and on his home debut Town thrashed hapless West Brom 7–0. Mariner was on target, but the star of the show was his strike partner Trevor Whymark, who scored four times.

Mariner's arrival, coupled with John Wark establishing himself as a goalscoring midfielder, saw Town enjoy a much-improved season. They finished third in Division One, a single point behind champions Liverpool.

Division One final position: Third

FA Cup: Fourth round

League Cup: Second round

Queen's Park Rangers had finished runners-up in Division One in 1975–76, being pipped by Liverpool by a single point. So a 2–2 draw at Portman Road in August 1976 was not a bad result for Town. Town's goals were an own-goal from visiting defender Ron Abbott and a Kevin Beattie penalty. In this picture, veteran Frank McClintock tackles Mick Lambert with Dave Clement in support.

With the departure of David Johnson to Liverpool, youngster Keith Bertschin was given his chance at the beginning of the 1976–77 season. He is seen here in action against Queen's Park Rangers in the 2–2 draw at Portman Road in August. However, Paul Mariner's big-money arrival in the autumn signalled the end of Bertschin's Ipswich career, and he was soon on his way to Birmingham City.

When Ipswich were drawn against Division Three Brighton in the second round of the League Cup in 1976, Town fans could be forgiven for thinking that their team would ease comfortably into the next round; however, football, as they say, is indeed a funny old game, and so it proved. The first game at Portman Road ended goalless, and the Seagulls shocked Town by winning 2–1 at the Goldstone Ground. Mick Lambert's goal failed to prevent the shock result. Here, Trevor Whymark is foiled by the Brighton defence in the first game at Portman Road.

A great study of Town's defensive kingpins, Allan Hunter and Kevin Beattie, in action against Brighton in the League Cup at Portman Road in August 1976. Hunter and Beattie did their jobs against the Division Three side – Town kept a clean sheet – but the Blues failed to score and Town went out in the away game.

Trevor Whymark in action against Leicester City at Portman Road in September 1976. The game ended goalless.

Town fans look less than enthralled during the game against Leicester at Portman Road in September 1976. You cannot blame them – it ended goalless.

Well, you were warned! Here's Roger Osborne celebrating after scoring against Arsenal in a League game at Portman Road in September 1976. While Osborne is congratulated by Clive Woods and Trevor Whymark, Arsenal players Liam Brady (number eight), Sammy Nelson, Pat Rice and David O'Leary seem to be conducting an inquest. All four were on duty in May 1978, when Osborne scored against them once more to win the FA Cup. Town won this game 3–1, with Eric Gates and Kevin Beattie (penalty) the other scorers.

Clive Woods and Eric Gates appear to have no opposition to contend with in this 3–1 win against Arsenal at Portman Road in September 1976. Gates was to effectively take Woods's place in the Town team, but not before Clive had enjoyed a fantastic afternoon at Wembley in 1978. In the background is World Cup-winner Alan Ball.

Two Clive Woods goals secured a 2–0 away win against West Ham in October 1976. Here, Roger Osborne shields the ball from Kevin Lock, with Kevin Beattie on hand.

A red letter day for Ipswich Town as Paul Mariner arrives at Portman Road in October 1976, after a lengthy, three-way battle for his signature from Plymouth. From left are Argyle manager Tony Waiters, Bobby Robson, Mariner and his then wife Alison.

Paul Mariner signs on the dotted line as he joins Town – a massive signing for Bobby Robson. Either side of Mariner are John Peddelty and Terry Austin who both joined Plymouth as part of the deal. Peddelty's career was cut short by a serious head injury, and he returned to Suffolk to become a policeman.

A memorable afternoon at Portman Road for a number of reasons. Ipswich annihilated West Bromwich Albion 7–0 in November 1976, equalling the club's record score. And one of the scorers was Paul Mariner, with his first goal for Town. Trevor Whymark scored four times, with John Wark and Kevin Beattie also on target. Here, Whymark helps Mariner celebrate his first strike for the Blues.

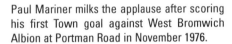

Paul Mariner milks the applause after scoring his first Town goal against West Bromwich Albion at Portman Road in November 1976.

Town fans pictured before the home game against West Bromwich Albion in November 1976. What a treat awaited them – Ipswich won 7–0, with Trevor Whymark getting four and Paul Mariner opening his account.

Allan Hunter is joined by his mate Kevin Beattie as he prepeares for his 250th Town game in November 1976. The big Irishman was to pass the 350-game mark before ending his Town career. Hunter, who joined Ipswich in 1971, was generally regarded as the best centre-half in Britain for a spell in the early 1970s.

Kevin Beattie is congratulated by his teammates after scoring in Town's 3–1 win over Sunderland at Portman Road in November 1976. The other scorers were Trevor Whymark and George Burley – a rare goal indeed from the Scottish full-back.

By 1976–77 Kevin Beattie's knee problems were beginning to plague him. They would eventually end his career. But in 1976 he was still a powerhouse, as he shows here in the 2–0 win against Middlesbrough in November. Paul Mariner and Brian Talbot were the scorers.

Paul Mariner turns away in triumph after scoring Town's first goal in a 2–0 win at Middlesbrough in November 1976. Brian Talbot scored the other goal.

Paul Mariner is in the midst of a happy huddle after scoring Town's winner in a 1–0 win over Liverpool at Portman Road in December 1976. Town's new boy was well on his way to being an Ipswich hero.

Ipswich boy Brian Talbot was a key man in his home-town team's successful side from the mid-1970s. Here he is, taking on Liverpool's Emlyn 'Crazy Horse' Hughes in this clash at Portman Road in December 1976. Town won this game 1–0, with a goal from Paul Mariner, but the Merseysiders had the last laugh, winning the League Championship – finishing just one point ahead of runners-up Manchester City and third-placed Ipswich. So near, yet so far.

Clive Woods has just scored the winning goal against visitors Manchester United in January 1977. Martin Buchan is appealing for something. Buchan's defensive partner Brian Greenhoff generously scored Town's other goal in a 2–1 victory.

Town beat Bristol City 4–1 in the FA Cup third round in 1977. Trevor Whymark is seen here celebrating his goal. Paul Mariner, also pictured, scored twice, with Eric Gates getting the other.

Four Town legends captured in one photograph: Paul Mariner has just scored against Bristol City in the FA Cup third round tie at Portman Road in 1977. Mariner gets a big hug from Kevin Beattie, while Trevor Whymark and Brian Talbot head back to the halfway line.

A sight Town fans would enjoy many times over the years. Paul Mariner celebrates one of his goals against Bristol City in the FA Cup third-round tie at Portman Road in 1977. Mariner scored twice in a 4–1 win.

Cheers! Bobby Robson at the refurbished Washbrook Inn in January 1977.

It does not look hopeful, does it? Norwich manager John Bond strides purposefully off the pitch at Portman Road as Cyril Lea, the referee, and Bobby Robson perform an impromptu ice dance during a pitch inspection in January 1977. The game did not go ahead.

John Wark has just scored from the spot and Town are on their way to a thumping 5–0 win over Norwich at Portman Road in February 1977. Norfolk boy Trevor Whymark helped himself to a hat-trick and Paul Mariner got the other one.

Eric Gates in action during a memorable night at Portman Road as Town beat Norwich 5–0 in February 1977.

Town skipper Mick Mills emptying a charity bottle at the Griffin pub in Yoxford, in February 1977. Note the Watneys Special Mild on offer.

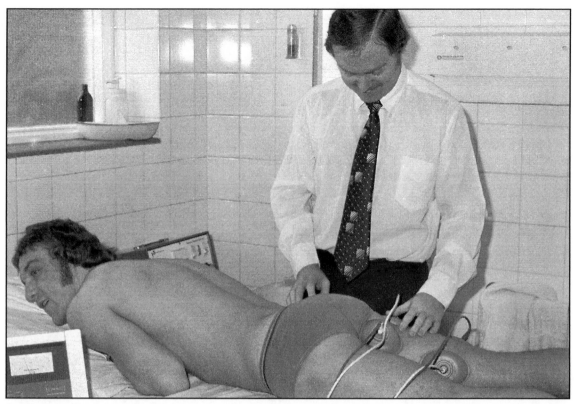

An all-too-familiar sight as the 1970s went on – Kevin Beattie on the treatment table. From the mid-1970s, 'The Beat' played fewer and fewer games as injuries took their toll. It was a crying shame: at his peak, Beattie was being compared with the Manchester United 'Busby Babe' Duncan Edwards, who died after the 1958 Munich air disaster. As it turned out, Beattie won only nine England caps. He should have had 100. Physio Brian Simpson is administering the treatment.

Young and old alike wrap up against the cold as Town take on Stoke at Portman Road in February 1977. The game did not warm them up – Stoke won 1–0.

Norfolk boy Trevor Whymark had a habit of scoring important goals against Norwich City. This game, at Carrow Road in April 1977, was no exception – Whymark scored the only goal. Here, we see Brian Talbot and Tony Powell perform a rather fetching dance routine. Martin Peters is in the background.

The two teams applaud Colin Viljoen on to the pitch at Portman Road before his testimonial game in May 1977. Viljoen had joined Ipswich under Bill McGarry and had progressed to win two England caps. After this game, Viljoen had one more, largely unhappy, season at Portman Road. In the Norwich line-up was a certain Martin Peters, who 11 years earlier had been busy winning the World Cup with England.

1977–78: Wembley glory

6 May 1978 will forever be one of the most memorable dates in Ipswich Town's history. It was on that sunny spring afternoon that unfancied, injury-hit Town, saw off firm favourites Arsenal in a totally one-sided FA Cup Final. Suffolk boy Roger Osborne might have scored the only goal, but the truth is that it was a 1–0 massacre. Mariner and Wark (twice) rattled the woodwork and Burley forced a wonder save from Arsenal 'keeper Pat Jennings as Town dominated from start to finish. The result sparked unforgettable scenes of celebration in Suffolk as the heartbreak of the semi-final defeat three years earlier was forgotten.

Ironically, Town had endured their worst League season for many years. They finished a lowly 18th, as injuries to key players took their toll. Beattie, Wark and Whymark all missed big chunks of the season, with Whymark sitting out the Cup Final. Town also enjoyed a run in the UEFA Cup, before cruelly being eliminated on penalties by Spanish giants Barcelona.

Young defenders Terry Butcher and Russell Osman played their first games for Town in this season.

Division One final position: 18th

FA Cup: Winners

League Cup: Fourth round

UEFA Cup: Third round

It's the opening day of the 1977–78 season, and David Geddis scores the only goal of the game as Town entertain Arsenal at Portman Road. Pat Jennings has no chance. It was Geddis's first goal for Ipswich. Much later in the season, the young striker would play a crucial role in a much more high-profile clash between Ipswich and the Gunners.

Brian Talbot celebrates his winning goal against Chelsea in August 1977. It was a rare bright spot in the League for Town, who finished a lowly 18th in Division One. At one point, it looked like Ipswich would be dragged into the relegation zone, especially after five consecutive League defeats early in the year. But they scraped together enough points to secure safety. Of course, minds were focused on another prize.

Despite the best efforts of Paul Cooper and Mick Mills, Kenny Dalglish puts Liverpool ahead in the League clash between Ipswich and Liverpool at Portman Road in September 1977. Ray Kennedy watches in admiration. However, Town did equalise through Trevor Whymark to grab a point.

It is 5 November 1977, and young Town players Russell Osman and David Geddis are trying to create fireworks against visitors Manchester City. Their opponent here is Mike Doyle. Town won the game 1–0 with a goal from Paul Mariner.

Brian Talbot has just scored against Leicester City at Filbert Street in November 1977. But this was just a consolation goal, as The Foxes won the game 2–1.

He went that way! Clive Woods ties an Everton defender in knots during the 3–3 draw at Portman Road in November 1977. Trevor Whymark scored twice, one from the penalty spot, with Paul Mariner getting the other.

Whenever the England manager's job became available – as it did quite regularly during the 1970s – Bobby Robson's name was inevitably in the frame. Here is one of those times, from 1977, when Robson has been intercepted by the television cameras. As always, he has found time for a few words. The interviewer is a very young Steve Rider.

The teams walk on to the pitch at Portman Road for the Ipswich v Barcelona UEFA Cup game in November 1977. Leading the Ipswich team is captain Mick Mills. Ipswich won the match 3–0 in front of a crowd of 33,663. The goal scorers were Eric Gates, Trevor Whymark, and Brian Talbot.

What a memory for the mascot as he meets the world's greatest footballer. Johann Cruyff shakes a very lucky little boy's hand as Town prepare to take on mighty Barcelona in the third round of the UEFA Cup at Portman Road in November 1977. Ipswich won this game 3–0, with goals from Eric Gates, Trevor Whymark and Brian Talbot. Cruelly, they lost the second leg by the same scoreline before going out of the competition on penalties.

Trevor Whymark was one of Town's goalscorers in the thumping 3–0 home-leg win against Barcelona. Heartbreak was to follow, though.

This is a rare sight – an injured Mick Mills. The Town skipper is recovering in hospital, and has a slightly embarrassed-looking visitor in the form of young reserve John Stirk. Once he got back to the action, Mills enjoyed a productive season in front of goal. Playing quite often in midfield in an injury-ravaged team, Mills netted no fewer than eight times, including most memorably in the FA Cup semi-final against West Bromwich Albion.

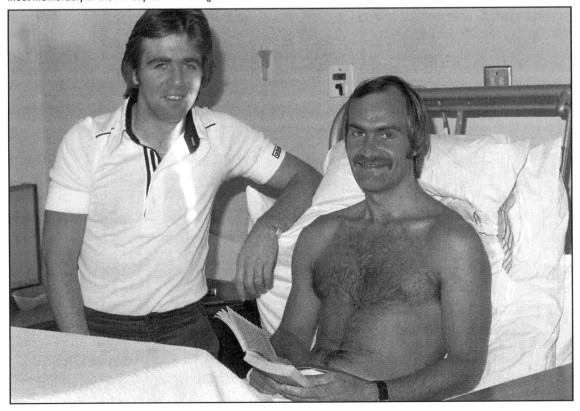

Paul Cooper and Allan Hunter in action against Arsenal at Highbury in January 1978. Although Town lost this game 1–0, revenge would be sweet later in the season.

Russell Osman keeps the Arsenal striking duo of Alan Sunderland and Malcolm Macdonald at bay in the game at Highbury in January 1978. Town lost the game 1–0, with unsung midfielder David Price scoring the only goal.

Robin Turner puts Brendon Batson under pressure during the 2–2 draw between Town and West Bromwich Albion at Portman Road in February 1978. Mick Mills and John Wark were the scorers. Turner spent the best part of a decade on the fringes of the first-team squad, filling in whenever one of the first-choice strikers was injured. He played a significant part in Town's 1978 Cup run, scoring both goals at a snowbound Eastville as Ipswich escaped with a fortunate 2–2 against Bristol Rovers in the fifth round.

John Wark begins his trademark celebration after scoring in the 2–2 home draw with West Bromwich Albion in March 1978. Mick Mills was Town's other scorer. A few weeks later, Wark would score a much more important goal against the Midlanders.

Town sailed through their FA Cup quarter-final match against Millwall 6–1, with Paul Mariner grabbing a hat-trick and the other goals coming from George Burley, John Wark, and Brian Talbot. Sadly, the headlines in the following day's papers barely mentioned the score. The stories were all about the shocking violence on the terraces as Millwall fans attacked Town supporters. In this picture, policemen struggle to restore order.

Robin Turner is thwarted this time by Millwall 'keeper Nicky Johns, but it really did not matter as Town thrashed the home side 6–1 to reach the FA Cup semi-final.

Paul Mariner celebrates one of his hat-trick goals in the FA Cup quarter-final at Millwall. Ex-Town player Bryan Hamilton looks less then pleased.

A bright spot in an otherwise disappointing League season. Town beat Norwich 4–0 at Portman Road in March 1978, with goals from Brian Talbot (two), David Geddis and Mick Mills. This picture shows Geddis apparently performing tricks with the ball, watched by Canaries defender Tony Powell.

High jinks in the Highbury dressing room after Town's 3–1 win over West Bromwich Albion in the FA Cup semi-final. Physio Tommy Egglestone is the man in the middle, apparently being given some terrible concoction by Bobby Robson!

We are all going to Wembley! George Burley, Roger Osborne, John Wark and Mick Lambert enjoying their bath after Town's FA Cup semi-final victory over West Bromwich Albion at Highbury.

Allan Hunter enjoys a cigarette after Town's FA Cup semi-final against West Brom. Kevin Beattie and Robin Turner are also in celebratory mood.

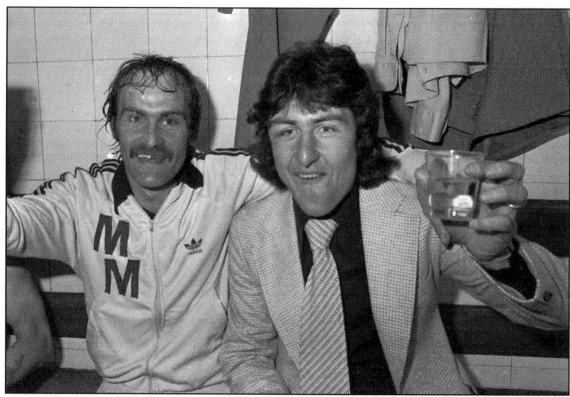

Brian Talbot's right eye is a bit of a sight, but who cares? Talbot suffered the injury when bravely heading Town in front in the FA Cup semi-final against West Bromwich Albion. Mick Mills, also a goalscorer on the day, helps Talbot to celebrate.

6 May 1978, and it is the biggest day in the history of Ipswich Town Football Club with a trip to Wembley for the FA Cup Final against Arsenal. This picture shows the Osborne Express, as Roger Osborne's family get ready to board their coach to Wembley. What a day they would enjoy, with their boy scoring Town's most famous goal.

Bobby Robson's favourite dish – Bacon and Eggs. That is what he nicknamed the defensive duo of Allan Hunter and Kevin Beattie after Town's Wembley triumph. Both were injury doubts leading up to the match, but there was never any real chance of either missing out! Both performed brilliantly on the day.

A great deal of hard work and thinking time went into the creation of the array of banners which Ipswich fans held aloft at the tunnel end at Wembley on 6 May 1978. Some them were less than politically correct!

Ipswich rule Wembley, says the poster – and it came true.

A perfectly timed Mick Mills tackle stops Alan Sunderland in his tracks as Town head towards victory in the Cup Final. Sammy Nelson and referee Derek Nippard look on.

We are nearly there, lads. The inspirational Allan Hunter urges on his teammates as Town close in on victory at Wembley. Kevin Beattie looks remarkably relaxed about the whole thing.

A rare sight indeed – Clive Woods heading the ball! This effort did not trouble Arsenal 'keeper Pat Jennings during the FA Cup Final, but with the ball at his feet Woods ran the Gunners defence ragged.

Brian Talbot is one step ahead of Arsenal's Alan Hudson in the FA Cup Final. Kevin Beattie is nearby. A year later, Talbot was a Cup winner again – this time with Arsenal.

Another Arsenal effort sails harmlessly past the post. Paul Cooper and Mick Mills are in charge of the situation, while future Town striker Alan Sunderland looks on helplessly. Sunderland would have a happier day out at Wembley the following May, when his last-gasp goal secured a 3–2 win for the Gunners over Manchester United.

It's THAT moment – the most famous goal in Ipswich Town's entire history. Roger Osborne has just swung his left boot, and the ball is on its way into the back of the Arsenal net, despite the best efforts of Pat Jennings – then one of the best goalkeepers in the world. Cue wild celebrations at the blue-and-white end of Wembley Stadium, and legendary status for Osborne, the unassuming local boy from Otley.

You beauty! Town 'keeper Paul Cooper celebrates Roger Osborne's Cup-winning goal.

'How long left, Ollie?'

This is *EADT/Evening Star* photographer Owen 'Ollie' Hines's famous photograph of Town 'keeper Paul Cooper as the minutes tick by at the end of the **1978 FA Cup Final.**

Goal hero Roger Osborne and Mick Mills with the FA Cup at Wembley.

Winners' medals in hand, the Town players salute their fans.

Blue-and-white heroes. The Town team after winning the FA Cup at Wembley. Included, in a suit, is Russell Osman, who was on standby to play if Allan Hunter had failed a fitness test on the morning of the match.

David Geddis was a surprise choice for the Cup Final team, but he performed superbly, setting up Roger Osborne's winning goal. Geddis wore the number-10 shirt, which in the match programme was listed as being Trevor Whymark's. It fooled future PM Margaret Thatcher who nominated the injured Whymark as her man of the match!

Hiya pal! Kevin Beattie spots a familiar face in the crowd at Wembley in 1978.

John Wark hit the same goalpost, in the same place, twice during the FA Cup Final. But it did not matter in the end, and here he is soaking up the post-match atmosphere.

Nice hats, lads! Allan Hunter and Kevin Beattie having a whale of a time after the Cup Final, with coach Cyril Lea.

The open-topped bus makes its way through the crowds in Ipswich town centre after Town's FA Cup victory.

Health and safety? Never heard of it, mate! Town fans find a rather precarious vantage point to join in the celebrations.

A delirious crowd packs the Cornhill in Ipswich as Town's Wembley heroes show off the FA Cup.

Ipswich supporters are crammed into every imaginable nook and cranny on the Cornhill in Ipswich as the celebrations get under way.

Bobby Robson shares the glory with the Mayor of Ipswich as the party carries on.

Roger Osborne looks suitably bashful as Bobby Robson holds him aloft during the celebrations at Ipswich Town Hall.

Local hero Roger Osborne enjoys the adulation at Ipswich Town Hall. With him are Clive Woods and coach Cyril Lea.

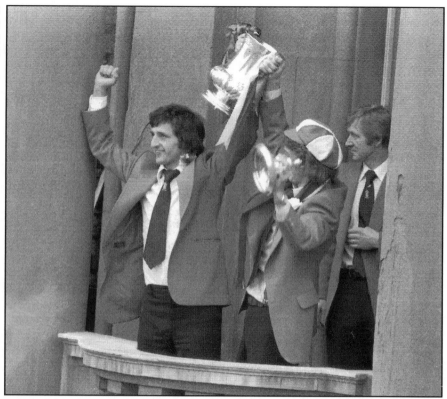

Goodness only knows what today's pampered Premier League millionaires would have made of Ipswich Town's schedule in the week after they won the FA Cup in 1978. First and foremost, the players had a right-old knees-up on the Saturday and Sunday. Then on the Monday evening, they played An Allstar XI at Portman Road in Mick Lambert's testimonial game, in front of nearly 17,000 fans. The following evening, everyone was back at Portman Road for the final League game of the season, against Wolves. Not surprisingly, Town lost 2–1. After a one-day break, Ipswich were off to Sudbury Town on the Thursday evening to play in a testimonial game for Malcolm Mackenzie. Then the following evening, Friday, Ipswich played Bury Town in a friendly at Ram Meadow. Here is a picture from that final evening, with goal hero Roger Osborne and Brian Talbot parading the Cup around a packed Ram Meadow.

1978–79: The Dutch masters

Although Town had captured the FA Cup, Bobby Robson showed his ambition and vision by transforming the team.

Most importantly, he ventured across the North Sea twice to capture the Dutch midfield duo Arnold Muhren and Frans Thijssen. With the arrival of the 'Dutch masters,' and the introduction on a more regular basis of youngsters Eric Gates, Alan Brazil, Terry Butcher and Russell Osman, the Town team was transformed in the space of a year.

The new-look line-up enjoyed a successful season, with Town qualifying for the UEFA Cup again by finishing sixth in the League. There was also excitement in two Cup competitions. Town reached the quarter-final of the Cup-Winners' Cup, before again losing to Barcelona, this time on the away goals rule. They also made it to the last eight of the FA Cup, before a 1–0 home defeat to Liverpool put the holders out.

Division One final position: Sixth

FA Cup: Quarter-final

League Cup: Second round

Cup-Winners' Cup: Quarter-final

The FA Cup winners proudly line up at the start of the 1978–79 season. But it was to be a year of transition, with some of the old faces fading out of the picture to be replaced by Russell Osman, Terry Butcher, and the two Dutchmen, Arnold Muhren and Frans Thijssen. It was the start of the rebuilding process which would culminate in the glorious 1980–81 season.

Paul Cooper looks round helplessly as Nottingham Forest celebrate one of their five goals in the FA Charity Shield Final at Wembley at the beginning of the 1978–79 season. It was a very unhappy return to Wembley for Cup-holders Ipswich, the weakened Suffolk side being beaten 5–0 by Brian Clough's League champions.

Town players troop off the pitch at Wembley after their 5–0 defeat to Nottingham Forest in the 1978 Charity Shield Final. The heavy defeat signalled a tough start to the season for Town, and it was only after Christmas that form really picked up, seeing the team finish in sixth place in Division One, qualifying for Europe once again. The growing influence of the two Dutchmen, Arnold Muhren and Frans Thijssen, was a major factor in the improved form.

The beginning of an exciting new era, as Arnold Muhren steps on to the turf at Portman Road to begin his illustrious Ipswich Town career. It was an inauspicious start. His debut, against Liverpool in August 1978, saw Town thumped 3–0 by the visitors, and Muhren spent most of the game watching the ball flying over his head as Ipswich resorted to long-ball tactics. Things would get a lot, lot better for the cultured Dutchman.

Kevin Beattie heads clear during Town's 3–0 victory over Manchester United at Portman Road in August 1978. Gordon McQueen (number five) is the Reds player closest to the action.

Kevin Beattie shakes off Manchester United striker Jimmy Greenhoff during Town's 3–2 win at Portman Road in August 1978. Paul Mariner scored twice, and Brian Talbot got the other. To today's young football fan, such a result would seem unimaginable. But back in those halcyon days, Ipswich were a better side than the mighty Reds.

There is a very famous face in the middle of this picture – Sky TV commentator Andy Gray, cunningly disguised by a mop of hair! Town lost this game against Aston Villa at Portman Road in September 1978 2–0.

Brian Talbot is congratulated by Kevin Beattie and Mick Mills after scoring one of Town's goals in the 3–0 win over Manchester United in August 1978.

Young fans celebrate a Town goal against AZ Alkmaar at Portman Road in September 1978. Having held the Dutch side to a goalless draw in the first leg in Holland, goals from Paul Mariner and John Wark (penalty) saw Town go through 2–0 after the home leg. The two sides would meet again, in the same competition, a couple of season later.

Paul Mariner is celebrating rather prematurely here, as John Wark slides in against Everton at Portman Road in October 1978. This was not a goal, and the Merseysiders won 1–0.

A young Alan Brazil in action against Everton in October 1978. Brazil scored his first goals for Ipswich in this season.

Paul Mariner watches as Russell Osman heads clear in the away leg of the UEFA Cup second-round game against SW Innsbruck in November 1978. Mariner was later sent off, but Town went through 2–1 on aggregate after a 1–1 draw in this game. George Burley scored the vital goal.

Russell Osman bravely tries to charge down a blockbuster from West Bromwich Albion striker Cyrille Regis in the game at Portman Road in November 1978. The visitors gained a tiny measure of revenge for their FA Cup semi-final defeat by winning this game 1–0.

Paul Mariner goes for the spectacular against Bolton at Portman Road just before Christmas 1978. Mariner was on target in a 3–0 win, the other scorers being Eric Gates and Brian Talbot. It was Ipswich-born Talbot's last goal for Town before his move to Arsenal.

Town's first opponents as they attempted to retain the FA Cup were Carlisle United, who came to Portman Road in the third round in January 1979. Ipswich won 3–2 and here's a special moment for Kevin Beattie as he scores against his home-town team. Paul Mariner is not having a lie down – he has just set up the goal on a snowbound pitch. Town's other goals came from Arnold Muhren and a John Wark penalty.

Yet another John Wark penalty successfully converted as the 'keeper dives out of the picture. This one was in a 3–1 win over Wolves at Portman Road in January 1979. Wark scored twice, with Paul Mariner getting the other.

Town beat visitors Wolves 3–1 in January 1979, with Paul Mariner scoring one and John Wark the other two. Mariner is seen here in aerial action. The unmistakeable figure of Wolves defender George Berry is also featured.

Leyton Orient came to Portman Road in the fourth round of the FA Cup in January 1979, and caused a mild shock when they held Town to a goalless draw. Everything was back on track in the replay at Brisbane Road, though – two Paul Mariner goals saw Ipswich through to the next round.

Everton 'keeper George Wood and the ball are both in the back of the net, and Paul Mariner is celebrating scoring the winner at Goodison in February 1979.

Scottish striker Alan Brazil made his big breakthrough in this season, scoring 11 times. Here he seems to be in pain during Town's 1–0 win over Everton at Goodison Park in February 1979. Paul Mariner scored the only goal of the game.

An iconic moment in the history of Ipswich Town Football Club as Arnold Muhren is joined by fellow Dutchman Frans Thijssen in February 1979. The 'Dutch Masters' would play a huge role for Town in the coming seasons.

Alan Brazil seems to be the only one celebrating during Town's home game against Nottingham Forest in March 1979. The other players – Trevor Francis, Russell Osman, and Larry Lloyd – look rather downbeat. Brazil scored Town's goal in this 1–1 draw.

Judging by how well the fans are wrapped up, it was obviously distinctly chilly when Town entertained Nottingham Forest in March 1979. Brian Clough's Forest, surprise League champions the season before, finished runners-up this time around.

Action from Ipswich v Nottingham Forest, March 1979. Paul Mariner jumps highest, with Mick Mills and Trevor Francis also attempting to get in on the action.

John Wark tries his luck against Coventry in March 1979. Warky failed to score during the 1–1 draw at Portman Road – Arnold Muhren was Town's goalscorer.

1979–80: Top three yet again

Another successful season, but frustratingly there was no silverware for the Portman Road trophy room.

Town finished third in Division One, yet again, although seven points behind Liverpool who were champions. The highlight of the League season came in March, when Town beat Manchester United 6–0 at Portman Road. Mariner helped himself to a hat-trick, Brazil scored twice, and Thijssen got the other. Town could even afford to miss two penalties!

There was another good run in the FA Cup, with Ipswich reaching the quarter-finals before going out by the odd goal in three against Everton at Goodison Park. The away goals rule again accounted for Town in the UEFA Cup, Grasshoppers of Zurich being the beneficiaries this time.

Better things were just around the corner…

Division One final position: Third

FA Cup: Quarter-Final

League Cup: Second round

UEFA Cup: Second round

The Ipswich Town first-team squad for the 1979–80 season. It was a curious season in many ways, with a poor start followed by a storming finish seeing Town finish third in Division One. They also reached the quarter-final of the FA Cup, before losing at Everton. Paul Mariner was top scorer with 22 goals.

It is the dreaded pre-season training again, lads! Clive Woods, Mick Mills and Allan Hunter show a rather unsure-looking Frans Thijssen the way. This is Alderman Road recreation ground, in the shadow of Ipswich Town's stadium, on a hot day in July 1979.

Chacteristically, Bobby Robson looks one of the more enthusiastic as the Town squad gets stuck into pre-season training in the summer of 1979.

Cup Final hero Roger Osborne is in the thick of the action here against Everton at Portman Road in September 1979. The game ended 1–1, with John Wark on target for Town. Ipswich lost their next five games.

Arnold Muhren was never blessed with great pace, but with a left foot like that who needs pace? Here is the master midfielder setting up yet another Town attack in the 1–1 home draw against Everton in September 1979.

Action from a little-remembered game between Town and New Zealand at Portman Road in October 1979. Ipswich won the match 1–0, but fewer than 2,000 diehards bothered to turn out.

You have got no chance, Craig! Liverpool's Craig Johnston should have realised he was wasting his time trying to prise the ball away from master dribbler Frans Thijssen. Mind you, Johnston had the last laugh in this game at Portman Road in October 1979 – Liverpool won 2–1, one of five consecutive defeats for Ipswich. Paul Mariner scored the consolation goal.

Beattie is back! 'The Beat' has just scored with a rocket shot against Grasshoppers of Zurich in the second round of the UEFA Cup at Portman Road in November 1979. Sadly, though, the game ended 1–1 and Town went out of the competition on away goals after a goalless draw in Switzerland.

Spot the Town legends: the pair walking behind Bobby Robson before the start of his Testimonial Game in 1979 are none other than Ted Phillips and Ray Crawford, who terrorised defences the length and breadth of the country as Alf Ramsey's unfancied team shocked the footballing world by winning the Division One title at the first attempt in 1962. No wonder 'Big' Ron Atkinson looks apprehensive.

More than 23,000 of the Ipswich faithful turned out for Bobby Robson's Testimonal Game at Portman Road in November 1979. Town played against an England XI, and the game ended 2–2. The most striking images from the occasion are those of a certain George Best turning out in a Town shirt!

Alan Brazil celebrates scoring in the Bobby Robson Testimonal in November 1979, when Town took on an England XI. Paul Mariner and someone called George Best are in the background.

The ultimate club stalwart, Mick Mills played his 600th game for Ipswich Town at the end of 1979. He went on to feature no fewer than 741 times for the Blues – a record that will almost certainly never be broken.

Bobby Robson and Arnold Muhren demonstrating their skills to youngsters at Westbourne School in Ipswich shortly before Christmas 1979.

After a very shaky start, including five consecutive League defeats in September and October 1979, Ipswich hit a golden vein of form which eventually carried them to third spot in the table. Arnold Muhren played a key role in another successful season, not only creating countless goals but also scoring six himself. Here is one of them, in the 3–1 home win against Spurs a few days before Christmas. Chris Hughton is the defender trying in vain to block the Dutchman's shot. Eric Gates and Paul Mariner were also on target. The conditions do not look great!

The Carrow Road 'leg' of the East Anglian derby was an absolute cracker. On Boxing Day 1979, Town and the Canaries fought out a 3–3 draw. Here is Eric Gates scoring one of Town's goals. The other Ipswich scorers were Arnold Muhren and John Wark. World Cup-winner Martin Peters is one of the Norwich players. On the scoresheet for Norwich that day was Alan Taylor, who had broken Town hearts four years earlier when he scored both goals for West Ham in the FA Cup semi-final.

Are you sure that is wise, Greg? Terry Butcher looks like he has been left for dead by Norwich City's Greg Downs in the 3–3 draw at Carrow Road on Boxing Day 1979. Hard man Terry would not have been amused by that!

Printed in Great Britain
by Amazon.co.uk, Ltd.,
Marston Gate.